Company Success in Manufacturing Organizations

A Holistic Systems Approach

T0384152

Industrial Innovation Series
Series Editor
Adedeji B. Badiru
Air Force Institute of Technology (AFIT)—Dayton, Ohio

PUBLISHED TITLES

Carbon Footprint Analysis: Concepts, Methods, Implementation, and Case Studies, *Matthew John Franchetti & Defne Apul*

Cellular Manufacturing: Mitigating Risk and Uncertainty, *John X. Wang*

Communication for Continuous Improvement Projects, *Tina Agustiady*

Computational Economic Analysis for Engineering and Industry, *Adedeji B. Badiru & Olufemi A. Omitaomu*

Conveyors: Applications, Selection, and Integration, *Patrick M. McGuire*

Culture and Trust in Technology-Driven Organizations, *Frances Alston*

Global Engineering: Design, Decision Making, and Communication, *Carlos Acosta, V. Jorge Leon, Charles Conrad, & Cesar O. Malave*

Global Manufacturing Technology Transfer: Africa–USA Strategies, Adaptations, and Management, *Adedeji B. Badiru*

Guide to Environment Safety and Health Management: Developing, Implementing, and Maintaining a Continuous Improvement Program, *Frances Alston & Emily J. Millikin*

Handbook of Emergency Response: A Human Factors and Systems Engineering Approach, *Adedeji B. Badiru & LeeAnn Racz*

Handbook of Industrial Engineering Equations, Formulas, and Calculations, *Adedeji B. Badiru & Olufemi A. Omitaomu*

Handbook of Industrial and Systems Engineering, Second Edition, *Adedeji B. Badiru*

Handbook of Military Industrial Engineering, *Adedeji B. Badiru & Marlin U. Thomas*

Industrial Control Systems: Mathematical and Statistical Models and Techniques, *Adedeji B. Badiru, Oye Ibidapo-Obe, & Babatunde J. Ayeni*

Industrial Project Management: Concepts, Tools, and Techniques, *Adedeji B. Badiru, Abidemi Badiru, & Adetokunboh Badiru*

Inventory Management: Non-Classical Views, *Mohamad Y. Jaber*

Kansei Engineering—2-volume set

- Innovations of Kansei Engineering, Mitsuo Nagamachi & Anitawati Mohd Lokman
- Kansei/Affective Engineering, Mitsuo Nagamachi

Kansei Innovation: Practical Design Applications for Product and Service Development, *Mitsuo Nagamachi & Anitawati Mohd Lokman*

Knowledge Discovery from Sensor Data, *Auroop R. Ganguly, João Gama, Olufemi A. Omitaomu, Mohamed Medhat Gaber, & Ranga Raju Vatsavai*

Learning Curves: Theory, Models, and Applications, *Mohamad Y. Jaber*

Managing Projects as Investments: Earned Value to Business Value, *Stephen A. Devaux*

Modern Construction: Lean Project Delivery and Integrated Practices, *Lincoln Harding Forbes & Syed M. Ahmed*

Moving from Project Management to Project Leadership: A Practical Guide to Leading Groups, *R. Camper Bull*

Project Management: Systems, Principles, and Applications, *Adedeji B. Badiru*

Project Management for the Oil and Gas Industry: A World System Approach, *Adedeji B. Badiru & Samuel O. Osisanya*

Quality Management in Construction Projects, *Abdul Razzak Rumane*

Quality Tools for Managing Construction Projects, *Abdul Razzak Rumane*

Social Responsibility: Failure Mode Effects and Analysis, *Holly Alison Duckworth & Rosemond Ann Moore*

Statistical Techniques for Project Control, *Adedeji B. Badiru & Tina Agustiady*

STEP Project Management: Guide for Science, Technology, and Engineering Projects, *Adedeji B. Badiru*

Sustainability: Utilizing Lean Six Sigma Techniques, *Tina Agustiady & Adedeji B. Badiru*

Systems Thinking: Coping with 21st Century Problems, *John Turner Boardman & Brian J. Sauser*

Techonomics: The Theory of Industrial Evolution, *H. Lee Martin*

Total Productive Maintenance: Strategies and Implementation Guide, *Tina Agustiady & Elizabeth A. Cudney*

Total Project Control: A Practitioner's Guide to Managing Projects as Investments, Second Edition, *Stephen A. Devaux*

Triple C Model of Project Management: Communication, Cooperation, Coordination, *Adedeji B. Badiru*

FORTHCOMING TITLES

3D Printing Handbook: Product Development for the Defense Industry, *Adedeji B. Badiru & Vhance V. Valencia*

Company Success in Manufacturing Organizations: A Holistic Systems Approach, *Ana M. Ferreras & Lesia L. Crumpton-Young*

Design for Profitability: Guidelines to Cost Effective Management of the Development Process of Complex Products, *Salah Ahmed Mohamed Elmoselhy*

Essentials of Engineering Leadership and Innovation, *Pamela McCauley-Bush & Lesia L. Crumpton-Young*

Handbook of Construction Management: Scope, Schedule, and Cost Control, *Abdul Razzak Rumane*

Company Success in Manufacturing Organizations

A Holistic Systems Approach

Dr. Ana Ferreras
National Academy of Sciences

Dr. Lesia Crumpton-Young
Tennessee State University

CRC Press
Taylor & Francis Group
Boca Raton London New York

CRC Press is an imprint of the
Taylor & Francis Group, an **informa** business

CRC Press
Taylor & Francis Group
6000 Broken Sound Parkway NW, Suite 300
Boca Raton, FL 33487-2742

First issued in paperback 2021

ISBN 13: 978-0-367-78200-9 (pbk)
ISBN 13: 978-1-4822-3317-9 (hbk)

Library of Congress Cataloging-in-Publication Data

Names: Ferreras, Ana, author. | Crumpton-Young, Lesia, author.
Title: Company success in manufacturing organizations : a holistic systems
approach / Ana Ferreras, Lesia Crumpton-Young.
Description: 1 Edition. | Boca Raton, FL : CRC Press, [2017] | Series:
Industrial innovation series
Identifiers: LCCN 2017011446| ISBN 9781482233179 (hardback : alk. paper) |
ISBN 9781482233186 (ebook)
Subjects: LCSH: Success in business. | Employee motivation. | Industrial
efficiency.
Classification: LCC HF5386 .F4127 2017 | DDC 658--dc23
LC record available at https://lccn.loc.gov/2017011446

Visit the Taylor & Francis Web site at
http://www.taylorandfrancis.com

and the CRC Press Web site at
http://www.crcpress.com

Contents

Preface

This book presents a complete guide for corporate leaders to make better decisions in highly dynamic and complex business environments where many factors must be taken into account. The guide presents a company success index model that can be easily implemented by manufacturing companies to monitor the organizational performance and continuously improve their profit, productivity, efficiency, quality, ergonomics and safety, and employee morale. The core of this book is a unique approach to measure success using a multifaceted and holistic methodology that encompasses critical areas for any manufacturing business to lead the market.

The book describes a series of models that assist organizational leaders in making good decisions in complex situations where many factors are simultaneously changing and affecting company performance. Companies have been collecting data for decades at different levels of the organization but many of them do not even analyze the data and if they do, they do not use it to make better decisions or improvements in the enterprise. Even though sufficient research studies have demonstrated the need to use more than financial measures, organizational decision makers have continued ignoring qualitative attributes when it comes to making holistic decisions. While many organizations are using some type of performance measurement approach, they remain without a methodology and a set of metrics capable of measuring company performance holistically.

Company leaders are in great need of a simple model that can assist them in monitoring company performance and making wise decisions to lead the market. While company leaders make decisions based on previous experiences, they would like to have a systemic approach, model, or tool that can assist them in evaluating company success holistically. Decision makers in business enterprises would like to have a tool that can not only assist them in predicting organizational performance, but also in comparing the enterprise against competitors. The uniqueness of this book is that in seven chapters, it provides the following:

- A valid and robust methodology that can be used by manufacturing companies to develop their own models
- A new quality model for managers to holistically measure quality success
- The first integrated approach for quantitatively modeling ergonomics and safety issues
- A new employee morale model, the Ferreras model
- A survey to calculate the Return on Investment in employee morale factors
- A company success index model where 64 quantitative and qualitative performance measures are combined
- Guidance for organizational leaders to implement the aforementioned models in their enterprises and manufacturing plants
- Performance measures and metrics for every critical area of company success

This reference book is designed to prepare engineers or future organizational leaders and manufacturing managers to measure, monitor, and predict company success. It is also intended to help current or future ergonomics and safety managers, human resources leaders, and quality managers in measuring success in their areas and how that affects the overall enterprise success. The material is presented in a way that the critical components of company success and their performance measures are studied in detail. This book will walk the reader through the critical and diverse organizational areas required to measure company success in manufacturing organizations and the development of a holistic index model.

Acknowledgments

I would like to thank Dr. Lesia Crumpton-Young for the encouragement, guidance, and mentorship in writing this book. I would also like to thank my family for providing me unconditional love and support, and those friends who believed in me and the beauty of my dreams. Writing a book has taught me that discipline, constancy, willpower, patience, and perseverance are key strengths to achieve major career milestones. As Saint Francis of Assisi once said, "Start by doing what is *necessary*, then what is *possible*, and suddenly you are doing the *impossible*."

—**Ana Ferreras**

Authors

Dr. Ana Ferreras often serves as a speaker, professional developer, consultant, evaluator, researcher, fundraising expert, and advisor for organizational leaders in the private sector, academia, and federal government. Dr. Ferreras earned a PhD in industrial engineering and management systems (IEMS) from the University of Central Florida (UCF); her doctoral research focused on the development of mathematical models to assist organizational leaders in making wiser decisions in complex situations. She is one of the few industrial engineers in the United States working on science policy and science diplomacy. She is also a senior program officer at the National Academy of Sciences, Engineering, and Medicine where she manages the U.S. National Committees for theoretical and applied mechanics, physics, radio science, crystallography, and mathematics instruction. Dr. Ferreras also holds an MS in engineering management from the Florida Institute of Technology and a BS in electrical engineering from UCF. During her doctoral research, she assisted the IEMS Department at UCF in reengineering the undergraduate curriculum by developing a national model, new programs, experiential laboratories, and research centers/institutes. Prior to getting into science and engineering diplomacy, Dr. Ferreras was a winter 2008 Christine Mirzayan Policy Graduate Fellow with the Center for Advancement of Scholarship on Engineering Education at the National Academy of Engineering, Washington DC, USA. Email: corporate.performance.inc@gmail.com

Dr. Lesia Crumpton-Young, as vice president, serves as Tennessee State University's chief research officer responsible for the vision, direction, and guidance of the University's research mission and strategies for institutional advancement. She serves as the executive director of the TSU Research Economic and Community Development Foundation. She also heads the Institutional Advancement unit responsible for alumni affairs, alumni donations, corporate giving, and partnerships.

Dr. Crumpton-Young holds a PhD, an MS, and a BS in industrial engineering from Texas A&M University with a specialty area in human factors engineering. She has worked extensively as a professor, research scientist, CEO in the public sector, and university administrator at the University of Central Florida, Mississippi State University, and Texas A&M University, and as program director in the Education and Human Resource Directorate of the National Science Foundation. A prolific writer, Dr. Crumpton-Young has published and copublished many articles on engineering design, system modeling, engineering leadership, innovation, and STEM education.

chapter one

Company success in the twenty-first century

Manufacturing is nowadays considered the single most important industry (70%) for a country's economic health (Selko 2012). Company leaders— from the executive team down to the managers and shift supervisors of individual plants—have the power to give their organizations a true competitive advantage. Increasingly, winning companies will seize this opportunity and adapt their core beliefs, starting now (Hammer and Somers 2015).

Data analytics has become a well-known tool recently since more organizations are using it to know where they stand. *The Harvard Business Review* report published in 2012 titled *The Evolution of Decision Making: How Leading Organizations Are Adopting a Data-Driven Culture* presents a survey data and analysis of 646 executives, managers, and professionals, along with more than 10 in-depth interviews with individuals whose companies are at the forefront of adopting a data-driven culture. The survey finds that 11% of the responding organizations are in the group that has integrated analytics across the entire organization. While respondents' companies usually recognize the need to step up decision-making abilities, many do not have all processes in place to meet the challenge. For example, only a quarter of those in the survey have a formal, corporate-wide decision-making process. One-fifth says their decision-making processes are inconsistent or at best have an informal process. Survey respondents noted frustration with their organizations' current states on decision-making. Many respondents note that in addition to being able to make decisions faster, they are also making better decisions by using the tools in a data-driven culture. "The economy has become so competitive that you have to use analytics to compete," explains Christopher C. Williams, strategy executive of J. P. Morgan Chase. The companies that have moved to fact-based, evidence-based decision-making—which is honed against managerial instincts—are simply making decisions superior to those of the companies that still make decisions based on "gut feeling." Superior companies are doing something differently, which is building an ecosystem so executives understand all the linkages, connections, and historical bases for their decisions. These executives are making wiser and more strategic decisions today than ever (*Harvard Business Review* 2012). Data-driven decision making gives corporate leaders a greater chance to make wiser decisions based on evidence-based and company performance.

1.1   What drives success?

PwC Strategy& developed a web-based survey in 2013 where 720 executives selected up to three public companies within their industry and commented on what drives success for those companies as well as their own company. The survey assessed the relationship between companies' approach to value creation and their performance. The participants also identified the main challenges companies face in strategy development and assessed the role that a strong identity plays in promoting a company's success. The survey found that there is no dominant strategy or school of strategy. Companies that owe their success to more asset-driven factors (economies of scale, lucrative assets, or diversification) have measurably lower performance. PwC states that what drives success is the importance of a clear identity and the top issues in strategic development. The survey found out that the common issues companies face in developing strategy are: (1) having too many strategic initiatives (29% respondents), and (2) focusing too much on short-term performance improvement and too little on what will create long-term success (27% respondents). Also, decision makers might select and pursue a bad strategy. Overall, only about one out of three respondents (36%) indicated that the top leaders of their companies were effective at both strategy development and execution, although both dimensions strongly correlate with company performance (Kleiner and Kubis 2013; Leinwand and Mainardi 2013).

Success is a complex achievement that cannot be evaluated or measured by looking into a single area or factor. Osborne and Gaebler (1992) stated:

1. If you don't measure results, you can't tell success from failure
2. If you can't see success, you can't reward it—and if you can't reward success, you are probably rewarding failure
3. If you can't recognize failure, you can't correct it

1.2   Manufacturing leaders and their complex decisions

Organizational decisions are made by the highest level of any business where leaders, top managers, and owners are commonly found. Corporate leaders deal with complex problems and decisions that significantly affect the company success. Organizational managers in manufacturing enterprises need more decision-making tools, methods, and techniques to measure company success and predict its future performance.

Organizational decisions continue to become more complex for top managers considering the large amount of poorly quantified qualitative performance measures that affect company success. Organizational decision makers frequently face high-risk decisions, which entail large and complex data as well as external factors that influence organizational success. Many organizational leaders do not measure critical performance measures essential to achieve company success or they fail to use the data collected to make better decisions. Understanding the significance and complexity of organizational performance measures can help to develop more realistic tools, methods, and techniques that combined can to assist organizational decision makers.

Decision makers for manufacturing companies are looking to gain better visibility into key performance indicators, both in the back office and on the manufacturing floor. After all, it is difficult, if not impossible, to improve processes that are not measured. For manufacturing companies, the pressures of the global economy require a constant commitment to establishing competitive advantages.

1.3 Decision-making in manufacturing organizations

These types of decisions are the most unstructured, uncertain, and risky, partly because they reach so far into the future that is hard to control them (Harris 1998).

Decisions should be made and evaluated at all the business levels, but unfortunately many organizations experience a large amount of decisions at the operational level, which indicates that not enough organizational thinking and planning has been previously performed (Harris 1998). This creates a reactive organization, responding to external forces around the business and never getting control of the organization. Customer satisfaction, supply change, environmental factors, and economic demands compel organizations to achieve a variety of objectives simultaneously, but often these objectives are in conflict.

Schiemann and Lingle performed in-deep research and studies on what they defined as measurement-managed organizations (Schiemann and Lingle 1999). In one of their studies performed in 1996, they studied 58 measurement-managed organizations versus 64 nonmeasurement-managed organizations and they found that 97% of measurement-managed organizations reported success with major change efforts—versus only 55% of nonmeasurement-managed organizations. In addition, similar differences were reported for being perceived as an industry leader over 3 years (74% vs. 44%) and being reported as financially ranked in the top third of their industry (83% vs. 52%) (Lingle and Schiemann 1996). Baltazar Herrera (2007) stated that today's organizational performance measures are financial and nonfinancial, qualitative and quantitative, and hard (financial and operating efficiency) and soft (customer satisfaction and employee engagement) (Teague and Eilon 1973).

1.4   *Toward a holistic characterization of company success*

Although company success has been financially characterized before, a reliable organizational performance methodology that provides a systematic measurement approach based on the company success components—profit, productivity, efficiency, quality, employee morale, safety and ergonomics—has never been developed. In addition, a holistic model to evaluate safety and ergonomics, quality, and employee morale has also been developed. Furthermore, a company success index model that encompasses a large amount of quantitative and qualitative performance measures is essential for manufacturing leaders. Considering the inevitable situation of dealing with qualitative data, different approaches are presented in this book to quantify qualitative measures and combine them with quantitative measures.

To achieve such a complex model, it is imperative to identify performance measures for profit, ergonomics, safety, employee morale, quality, efficiency, and productivity that represent company success in the manufacturing sector and develop a holistic index model that encompasses all these areas.

While business leaders frequently set up organizational goals, they do not have a holistic model that assists them in collecting and analyzing key performance measures systematically. Although there are many indices in the market that provide a ranked listing of organizations based on various criteria such as Fortune 500, which focuses on profit or the 100 Best Companies to Work For, which focuses on the employers' human capital, there is no company success index model that assesses and ranks organizations using a holistic approach.

There is a need for a new holistic approach that assists manufacturing leaders in measuring company performance systematically using quantitative and qualitative indicators. An approach that facilitates the measurement of key success factors and the understanding of their effect on the overall company success is highly needed. This book presents a new holistic index model to measure and predict company success in manufacturing organizations.

Profit, productivity, efficiency, quality, ergonomics and safety, and employee morale are critical components that greatly impact company success within organizations. Therefore, it is essential that a valid and reliable systematic approach that encompasses all of these factors is developed for use by top management in today's rapidly changing market environment. Organizational level decisions made based upon a single goal or narrow perspective that only considers one of the aforementioned components such as profit while ignoring others such as employee morale have proven harmful to the long-term viability and success of companies. Often, organizational leaders are not adequately equipped to consider multiple factors that are pertinent to company success due to the complexity associated with considering a large number of organizational variables and the lack of quantitative tools and techniques to assist them in the process. Thus, valid, reliable, and readily available tools, methods, and techniques for integrating multiple components of profit, ergonomics and safety, employee morale, quality, efficiency, and productivity into decision-making are highly needed in today's complex business environment. This book responds to the need for developing new quantitative models by using an approach to analyze and evaluate multiple factors essential for company success.

The key components of company success proposed in this book are illustrated in the following representation (Figure 1.1).

This reference book shows how the combine effect of profit, productivity, efficiency, quality, employee morale, ergonomics and safety affect

Figure 1.1 Components of company success.

company success in the manufacturing arena. It also presents a comprehensive literature review and a series of organizational success metrics to quantitatively and qualitatively measure organizational performance where a large number of interrelated factor variables are present.

This chapter provides an overview of the process of characterizing and measuring company success in the manufacturing sector. It also describes the great need for this work not only in manufacturing applications, but also in other sectors and industries.

Chapter 2 provides a reliable methodology and approach for organizational managers and manufacturing leaders to make wiser decisions and obtain company success. The methodology in Chapter 2 can be benchmarked by other organizations and applied to other type of applications, such as the service industry or government sector. In addition, this book presents a series of models, such as employee morale in Chapter 3, quality in Chapter 4, and ergonomics and safety in Chapter 5.

Chapter 3 presents an employee morale model and a survey that measures this complex component holistically using qualitative and quantitative performance measures. Also, a survey to prioritize employee morale improvements and investments based on the employees' willingness to pay is introduced. Research shows that a strong correlation exists between employee morale and profit. Gallup (2002) reports that companies with highly satisfied employees often exhibit above average levels of profitability (33%).

Chapter 4 introduces a unique quality model that uses quantitative and qualitative performance measures to assess it holistically. Measuring this key component from the producer and the user side is extremely important. Although 80% of companies say they deliver "superior" customer service, only 8% of the customers think these same companies deliver "superior" service. On average, loyal customers are worth up to 10 times as much as their first purchase, so the need to retain them in a very competitive market is essential for any business to succeed (Help Scout 2016).

An ergonomics and safety model is presented in Chapter 5 to assist human factors and safety managers in measuring, monitoring, and predicting ergonomics and safety in manufacturing organizations and how that impacts the business success. Medical costs in countries like the United States are high, which can seriously affect the success of any manufacturing businesses. It cannot be overlooked when businesses spend $170 billion a year on costs associated with occupational injuries and illnesses, which come straight out of company profits. However, workplaces that establish safety and health management systems can reduce their injury and illness costs by 20%–40%. In today's business environment, these costs can be the difference between operating in the black and running in the red. Lost productivity from injuries and illnesses costs companies

$60 billion each year. Safe environments improve employee morale, which often leads to increased productivity and better service (Occupational Safety & Health Administration [OSHA] 2016).

Furthermore, Chapter 6 summarizes profit, productivity, and efficiency. These areas are directly related to the previous chapters, and therefore they cannot be ignored. However, these three components have been modeled before using a holistic approach; therefore, there is no need to develop a Fuzzy model. Instead, a membership function is developed for each.

Finally, Chapter 7 presents a holistic company success index model capable of assessing and predicting organizational performance in manufacturing organizations using quantitative and qualitative measures. Case examples are presented through this book to illustrate the models and key membership functions.

This reference book is designed to assist manufacturing leaders and plant managers in making wiser decisions when confronting complex situations. This reading is intended to prepare future decision makers in measuring, monitoring, and predicting company success in manufacturing enterprises. This book also helps current or future managers in departments, such as human resources, quality, safety and ergonomics, to measure the success in their respective area/department, and the effects in the overall business success. Finally, this book shares new indicators, tools, methods, and techniques ready to be implemented. After reading this book, organizational decision makers, consultants, and academicians will be better equipped to make complex decisions and achieve organizational excellence, holistically. In addition, this book helps predict organizational success while providing a reliable performance measure methodology ready to be implemented by any manufacturing firm.

1.5   Limitations of previous approaches

This book characterizes company success in manufacturing organizations by focusing on the following six major components: profit, productivity, efficiency, quality, ergonomics and safety, and employee morale. The quantitative and qualitative performance measures and metrics presented in this book are generated after performing an extended literature review on existing research and Subject Matter Experts' opinion.

Historically, many tools, methods, and techniques have been developed to measure organizational performance; however, they all have limitations. In the past two decades, machine learning and artificial intelligence have become very popular disciplines to develop predicting models or optimize decisions. Genetic algorithms and neural networks are some of the most popular approaches used nowadays to develop dynamic models that can assist in making optimal decisions and analyzing a large amount of data. While these sophisticated and highly computational techniques offer new possibilities in the field of organizational management and decision-making, they require large data sets, which many organizations do not have. Data collection takes time and money, and many business leaders are not willing to invest a great deal of their resources in collecting and analyzing a large amount of data.

On the basis of the extensive research performed, the limitations of the existing organizational performance measurement systems are

- Mainly constructed as monitoring and controlling tools rather than decision-making or continuous improvement tools (Bititci et al. 2005)
- Current approaches do not provide a list of key performance measures and metrics
- Static systems
- Existing models do not predict, achieve, or improve future performance
- Organizational performance frameworks proposed do not provide mathematical models to simultaneously analyze key performance measures
- No model provides a systematic approach to continuously evaluate key performance measures (Bititci et al. 2005)
- Existing measurement tools require a large amount of data
- Current techniques identify the importance of qualitative data, but do not provide an approach to quantify it
- Existing techniques do not provide a standard list of organizational performance measures and metrics for manufacturing industries
- Effective organizational measurement systems must be consistent and definitions should be provided
- Metrics and measurement units must be clearly defined in order to succeed
- Although organizational performance frameworks have been proposed before, no mathematical modeling has been developed to simultaneously analyze multifaceted factor variables of manufacturing success
- No user-friendly measurement tool that can model and predict manufacturing success without a large amount of data (Medori and Steeple 2000)

References

Bititci, U., Mendibil, K., Martinez, V., and P. Albores. 2005. Measuring and managing performance in extended enterprises. *International Journal of Operations & Production Management*, 25, 333–353.

Gallup. 2002. *Creating a Highly Engaged and Productive Workplace Culture*. www.gallup.com

Hammer, M. and K. Somers. 2015. *Manufacturing Growth through Resource Productivity.* McKinsey&Company. March, http://www.mckinsey.com/business-functions/operations/our-insights/manufacturing-growth-through-resource-productivity

Harris, R. 1998. *Decision Making Techniques.* VirtualSalt. http://www.virtualsalt.com/crebook6.htm

Harvard Business Review. 2012. *The Evolution of Decision Making: How Leading Organizations are Adopting a Data-Driven Culture.* Harvard Business School Publishing, Copyright 2012. https://hbr.org/resources/pdfs/tools/17568_HBR_SAS%20Report_webview.pdf

Help Scout. 2016. *75 Customer Service Facts, Quotes & Statistics.* How your Business Can Deliver with the Best of the Best. Accessed September 3, 2016. https://www.helpscout.net/75-customer-service-facts-quotes-statistics/#eight

Herrera, B. M. 2007. *Integrating the Corporation: Management Metrics.* http://blog.360.yahoo.com/blogSuKwImc4dbIVkReBnskb6KWlMZkSn3QCwIbm?p=87

Kleiner A. and N. Kubis. 2013. PwC Strategy&. Strategy+Business. February 4. Accessed June 12, 2014. http://www.strategy-business.com/article/00165?gko=7a883

Leinwand, P. and C. Mainardi. 2013. *What Drives a Company's Success? Highlights of Survey Findings.* PwC Strategy&. Originally published by Booz & Company: October 28, 2013. Accessed September 10, 2016. http://www.strategyand.pwc.com/reports/what-drives-a-companys-success

Lingle, J. and W. Schiemann. 1996. From balanced scorecard to strategic gauges: Is measurement worth it? *Management Review,* 85, 56–61.

Medori, D. and D. Steeple. 2000. A framework for auditing and enhancing performance measurement systems. *International Journal of Operations & Production Management,* 20(5), 520–533.

Occupational Safety & Health Administration (OSHA). *U.S. Department of Labor.* Accessed September 3, 2016. https://www.osha.gov/Publications/safety-health-addvalue.html

Osborne, D. and T. Gaebler. 1992. *Reinventing Government: How the Entrepreneurial Spirit is Transforming the Public Sector.* (Reading, MA: Addison-Wesley Publishing Co.).

Schiemann, W. and J. Lingle. 1999. *Bullseye! Hitting Your Strategic Targets through High-Impact Measurement.* (New York, NY: The Free Press).

Selko, A. 2012. *What Makes a Manufacturing Company Competitive? Labor Productivity.* IndustryWeek. Aug. 6, http://www.industryweek.com/labor-employment-policy/what-makes-manufacturing-company-competitive-labor-productivity

Teague, J. and S. Eilon. 1973. Productivity measurement: A brief survey. *Applied Economics,* 5, 133–145.

chapter two

Modeling company success
A novel approach

2.1 The evolution of organizational performance measures

From the 1880s to the 1980s, financial measures such as profit, productivity, and return of investment dominated the performance measures environment, but the world market changed and the introduction of new manufacturing techniques such as Just in Time (JIT) or Total Quality Management (TQM) changed the traditional and obsolete performance measure perspective. Many researchers such as Banks and Wheelwright, Hayes and Garvin, and Kaplan have criticized financial indicators for leading and promoting short-term thinking since cost accounting focuses on minimization of variance rather than continuous improvement. Even though many organizational decision makers and manufacturing leaders are aware of the trade offs of using purely financial measures, a major proliferation of econometric models have been observed in the latest years such as Joseph Stiglitz in 2001 and Robert F. Engle III in 2003 (Bourne et al. 2000; Devitt 2001; Frängsmyr 2004).

Many studies performed in the 1980s suggest the necessity to pursue more nonfinancial measures to evaluate manufacturing organizations' performance. Financial performance measurements dominated the traditional manufacturing business, but company success spans far beyond the basic considerations of profit or Return on Investment (Banks and Wheelwright 1979; Hayes and Garvin 1982; Kaplan and Norton 1992; Amaratunga and Baldry 2002). Back in the days organizations were not collecting enough performance measures while nowadays they are measuring too many unfocused metrics. Considering the increase in performance measures observed in the latest years, it is no longer clear to many organizational leaders what the key competitive measures are and where the priorities lie (Neely et al. 2005; Busi and Bititci 2006). Frigo and Krumwiede reported that in the 5 years prior to 2000, around 50% of companies attempted to transform their organizational performance systems. By contrast, 85% of organizations planned to have performance measurement initiatives underway by the end of 2004 (Frigo and Krumwiede 1999). Business leaders need clear indicators for understanding how company success can be achieved in manufacturing environments. The integration of information on profit, productivity, efficiency, quality, employee morale, and ergonomics and safety performance measures will help in establishing a "common framework" or methodology to evaluate organizational performance and predict business success in manufacturing applications.

"It is important to realize that when a company is making a profit it does not necessarily imply that its operations, management and control systems are efficient" (Pollalis and Koliousis 2003: 7). Ghalayini and Noble in 1996 argued like Globerson in 1985 that profit or rate of return are not indicators of organizational success because such indicators do not help in identifying specific areas for improvement. Therefore, financial measures alone frequently mislead organizational decision makers to satisfactorily observe the key performance measures essential to achieve company success.

Wang Laboratories developed the SMART (Strategic Measurement Analysis and Reporting Technique) model, which consists of an integrated performance measurement system designed to sustain company success (Cross and Lynch 1989; Lynch and Cross 1991). The SMART system is characterized by a four-level performance pyramid which is represented by the vision of the organization within the top or highest level of the pyramid followed by the business units level or second level which consists of market measures and financial measures. The third level represents the business operating units and it is characterized by customer satisfaction, flexibility, and productivity while the fourth level represents departments and work centers which entails quality, delivery, process time, and cost.

The advantage of the SMART system is that it attempts to integrate corporate objectives with operational performance indicators, creating a feedback loop between the strategic level and the operational level. However, this system does not provide any mechanism to identify critical performance measures and metrics for the components described and ignores key performance measures related to human capital.

In the 1980s, Dixon developed the performance measurement questionnaire to help managers identifying organizational improvement needs and establish an agenda for performance measure improvements. Dixon's approach and questionnaire not only helps identifying the improvement areas of a company and the associated performance measures, but also evaluates if the existing measurement system supports the improvement efforts. This approach has been designed to identify inconsistencies between the current organizational performance measures and company strategy, but it fails to indicate how measures should be selected (Dixon et al. 1990).

In the 1990s, two economists from Harvard Business School, Robert S. Kaplan and David P. Norton, revolutionized the management world with the balanced scorecard (BSC) (Kaplan and Norton 1992). These economists identified the necessity of a broader list of performance measures aligned to the business vision leading to breakthrough improvements in performance. The dashboard or BSC is evaluated using financial and nonfinancial measurements in four major categories: financial, customer, internal, and learning/growth. Also, Kaplan and Norton's book *The Balanced Scorecard: Translating Strategy into Action* helped many international firms translate their strategy goals into performance measures (Kaplan and Norton 1996). Kaplan and Norton's original idea was to develop a company success measurement tool, but instead they created a strategic goal measurement tool (Kaplan and Norton 2002). The BSC provides an approach to identify organizational performance measures based on a company's strategy, but it fails to provide a standard list of organizational performance measures and metrics essential to succeed in the manufacturing sector. Also, this technique highly depends on the quality of the company leaders' vision (strategic level) to identify organizational performance measures; therefore, if company leaders have a narrow view or perspective, the organizational performance measures identified in the BSC will not appropriately capture the overall performance and health of the organization.

The Malcolm Baldrige award recognizes performance excellence within the quality field and its criteria has become a popular assessment tool. The Malcolm Baldrige National Quality Award was approved by President Reagan in 1982 as an effort to improve the level of productivity and quality across U.S. organizations (Evans and Lindsay 2002). The 2006 award criteria for the Malcolm Baldrige recognized business excellence based on seven categories: leadership, strategic planning, customer–market focus, information analysis, human resources focus, process management, and business results. The described criteria encourages any type of organization to enhance the company's competitiveness, by focusing in quality (Neely et al. 2005).

The European Foundation for Quality Management (EFQM) developed a model to achieve organizational excellence, and it was introduced as the European Quality Award criteria in 1992. The EFQM has become the most important quality excellence framework in Europe, just like the Malcolm Baldrige National Quality Award in the United States. The EFQM model of excellence has been widely used by many European organizations as a self-assessment tool to enhance organizational performance, and it presents a logical interpretation by grouping few areas as organizational "Enablers" (aim to pursue mission goals and objectives) and others as "Results" (real objective of the assessment). The EFQM model consists of nine criteria points: five are called "Enablers" (such as leadership—10%, people—9%, policy and strategy—8%, partnerships and resources—9%, and process—14%) and the other four are called "Results" (such as people results—9%, customer results—20%, society results—6%, and key performance results—15%). This model provides great criteria to achieve Quality Excellence through a feedback mechanism between Enablers and Results, but it fails to provide an organizational performance measures approach to achieve company success (Neely et al. 2005; Truccolo et al. 2005).

Sink and Tuttle characterized an overall company success model and approach in terms of performance measures in 1989 (Sink 1985; Sink and Tuttle 1989). The model identifies the complex interrelationship that exists between the following seven organizational performance areas: effectiveness, efficiency, quality, productivity, quality of work life, innovation, and profitability. Sink and Tuttle defined the seven performance areas as follows:

1. *Effectiveness* is the ratio of the actual output over the expected output or the capability to accomplish things right the first time. Some of the attributes commonly used to measure effectiveness are timeliness, quality, quantity, and price/cost.
2. *Efficiency* is the ratio of resources expected to be consumed over resources actually consumed. The same four attributes of timeliness, quality, quantity, and cost/price are often used to refine the measurement of efficiency.
3. *Quality* is a wide concept that is measured using the following five checkpoints: (1) the selection and management of upstream provider systems, (2) quality assurance, (3) in-process quality management, (4) outgoing quality assurance, and (5) proactive and reactive assurance that the organizational system is meeting or exceeding customer specifications.
4. *Productivity* is identified as the traditional ratio of output over input. Productivity has been viewed as having the strongest impact on performance, as well as giving insight into effectiveness, efficiency, and quality.
5. *Quality of work life* is the affective response of the people in the organizational system to any number of factors, such as their job, pay, benefits, working conditions, coworkers, supervisors, culture, autonomy, and skill variation.
6. *Innovation* is an important element to continuously improve or change whatever it takes to survive and grow; it also moderates the equation between productivity and profitability. Poor results in this area may also mean failure for an organization in the long term.
7. *Profitability* represents the relationship between revenues and costs (profit-center organizations) or *budgetability* (cost-center organizations), which represents the relationship between what the organizational system said it would do in terms of cost and the actual cost (Bourque et al. 2006).

Sink and Tuttle viewed the interrelationship between the seven performances criteria by focusing first on effectiveness, second on efficiency, and third on quality. Rolstadas stated that if these three concepts are in place, the result is very likely to be a productive organization (Rolstadas 1998). Quality of work life and innovation are viewed as moderators within this approach, so they can both increase and decrease performance. This organizational systems view approach supports the excellence of long-term outcomes, survival, and growth. Sink and Tuttle identified seven organizational performance areas as criteria to develop an objectives matrix with goals based on a multi attribute decision theory. Figure 2.1 captures the seven organizational performance areas described in the work of Sink and Tuttle.

Bourque et al. in 2006 considered the Sink and Tuttle approach to be a more comprehensive framework than the BSC, but they also considered that none of the existing models provide a mathematical framework for handling all the performance measures in an integrated manner. Therefore, Bourque et al. (2006) proposed a tool for multidimensional performance modeling for software engineering managers through the use of a genetic algorithm. This possibility of perusing a genetic algorithm or the application of neural networks was researched within an early stage of this research, but any of the described techniques requires a large data set which many organizations do not have or want to invest a large amount of money to develop. Fuzzy Set Theory (FST) models do

Figure 2.1 Organizational performance areas as described in the work of Sink and Tuttle.

not required a large amount of data leading to a more feasible approach for many manufacturing organizations. Table 2.1 summarizes the most influential practices in the evolution of performance measures and their trade offs.

While each of the approaches included in Table 2.1 helps to gain insights of measuring different business areas, these techniques do not provide a set of metrics to evaluate company success. Most of them rely on management and leadership to set a good strategic plan. The need to develop a holistic and multifaceted model that measures company success using quantitative and qualitative performance measures is an organizational decision-making priority for many manufacturing leaders.

Companies often struggle to integrate the key areas of company success. Lack of training in data collection, information inconsistencies, lack of data analysis, and data never used to make decisions are all consequences of having nonintegrated performance measurement systems. One of the major trends that companies are embracing nowadays is moving toward integrated human capital management approaches that provide better control over data and the ability to access centralized information from one dashboard (Bausch 2015).

In addition, the Engineering and Physical Sciences Research Council (EPSRC) funded the Integrated Performance Measurement Systems (IPMS) research program. EPSRC is the UK's main agency for funding research in engineering and the physical sciences. IPMS was built upon the BSC and EFQM models using a viable systems structure, which resulted in the development of the IPMS reference model (Bititci et al. 2005).

2.2   A new methodology

Although company success has been financially characterized before, a reliable methodology to measure and predict company success using profit, productivity, efficiency, quality, employee morale, and safety and ergonomics has never been developed before. Furthermore, quality, employee morale, and safety and ergonomics have never been holistically and quantitatively characterized or integrated within a company success index model.

Organizational decision makers continue to use more quantitative than qualitative data when making complex decisions because they do not tend to collect qualitative measures and if they do, they do not know how to combine them with the quantitative measures. Figure 2.2 shows the approach or methodology used to develop the Company Success index model that combines quantitative and qualitative performance measures.

Table 2.1 Overview of tools, methods, and techniques to measure organizational performance and business success

Tool, method, and technique	Purpose	Advantage	Disadvantage	Author
Strategic Measurement Analysis and Reporting Technique (SMART) developed by Wang Laboratories	To sustain company success	Integrates corporate objectives with operational performance indicators, creating a feedback loop between the strategic level and the operational level	Does not provide any mechanism to identify critical performance measures and metrics for the components described and ignores human capital key performance measures	Cross and Lynch (1989), Lynch and Cross (1991)
Performance measurement questionnaire	To identify the organizational improvement needs and establish an agenda for improvements in performance measure	Identifies inconsistencies between the current organizational performance measures and company strategy	Fails to indicate how the measures should be selected	Dixon et al. (1990)
Balanced score card (BSC)	To translate organizational strategy goals into performance measures	Provides an approach to identify organizational performance measures based on a company's strategy	Fails to provide a standard list of organizational performance metrics and depends on the company leaders' vision. No mathematical framework for handling all the performance measures in an integrated manner is identified	Kaplan and Norton (1992), Bourque et al. (2006)

(Continued)

Table 2.1 (Continued) Overview of tools, methods, and techniques to measure organizational performance and business success

Tool, method, and technique	Purpose	Advantage	Disadvantage	Author
Malcolm Baldrige National Quality Award	To recognize business excellence based on seven categories: leadership, strategic planning, customer–market focus, information analysis, human resources focus, process management, and business results	Encourages any type of organization to enhance a company's competitiveness	Only focus on quality	Evans and Lindsay (2002), Neely et al. (2005)
The European Foundation for Quality Management (EFQM) model	Used as a self-assessment tool to enhance organizational performance	Provides great criteria to achieve quality excellence through a feedback mechanism between enablers and results. Enablers (leadership—10%, people—9%, policy and strategy—8%, partnerships and resources—9%, and process—14%), Results (people results—9%, customer results—20%, society results—6%, and key performance results—15%)	Fails to provide an approach to achieve company success based on organizational performance measures	Truccolo et al. (2005), Neely et al. (2005)

(Continued)

Table 2.1 (Continued) Overview of tools, methods, and techniques to measure organizational performance and business success

Tool, method, and technique	Purpose	Advantage	Disadvantage	Author
The strategic performance improvement planning process	Interrelationships that exist among seven organizational performance areas: effectiveness, efficiency, quality, productivity, quality of work life, innovation, and profitability	Identifies the complex interrelationships that exist among seven organizational performance areas	It fails to identify a set of metrics to measure the seven organizational performance areas. Also, Bourque et al. (2006) commented that no mathematical framework for handling all the performance measures in an integrated manner is identified	Sink and Tuttle (1990)
The Integrated Performance Measurement Systems (IPMS)	Built upon the balance scorecard and EFQM models using the viable systems structure and resulted in the development of the IPMS reference model	The model underlines two main facets of the performance measurement system: *integrity and deployment.* This model is based on four levels (corporate, business units, business processes, and activities) and at each of these levels five key factors are considered (stakeholders, control criteria, external measures, improvement objectives, and internal measures)	It does not suggest performance measures or metrics; it is whatever the leadership identifies as objectives	Bititci et al. (1997), Institute of Management Accountants (1998), Garengo et al. (2005)

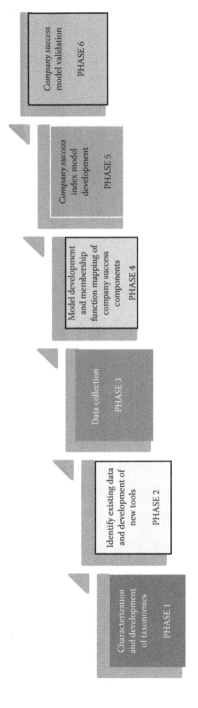

Figure 2.2 Research methodology.

2.2.1　Taxonomies development and key organizational performance measures: Step 1

This section describes the research performed in Step 1, which focuses on the development of taxonomies for all the company success components (profit, productivity, efficiency, quality, employee morale, and ergonomics and safety). The taxonomies developed characterize components, subcomponents, and factor variables affecting organizational success in the manufacturing industries. In addition, key organizational performance measures or metrics have been identified using various techniques, such as a literature review and subject matter experts (SMEs).

The purpose of developing taxonomies is to simplify and assist the characterization process when a complex problem needs to be solved. The taxonomy structure follows a configuration which facilitates the process of breaking a complex characterization problem into subcomponents, leading to a simplistic way to identify the key performance measures affecting company success.

To organizationally characterize the significant components, as well as the associated subcomponents, factor variables, and key performance measures, an extended literature review has been performed and validated by SMEs. In addition, a series of existing and new tools, methods, and techniques have been selected or developed within the following section in order to help evaluate the identified key performance measures for company success. Figure 2.3 illustrates the company success taxonomy, which entails six components key to attain company success in manufacturing organizations.

A taxonomy characterization has been developed for every component of the company success framework, which included organizational success subcomponents and factors variables identified after performing an extended literature review on key performance measures in manufacturing organizations. Moreover, subject matter experts from academia and industry have helped validate the taxonomies developed within this research.

2.2.2　Identify existing data and development of new tools: Step 2

The purpose of this step is to identify the existing tools, methods, and techniques that an organizational leader frequently uses, which could

Figure 2.3 Company success taxonomy overview.

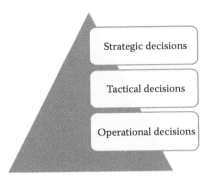

Figure 2.4 Levels of management information and decision system. (Guru99. 2016. Accessed December 1, 2016. http://www.guru99.com/mis-definition.html)

facilitate the organizational performance measures data collection process. As a result, an organizational leader questionnaire was developed in order to identify the decision-making challenges frequently encountered at the organizational level (see Appendix A). One of the main challenges is the fact that organizational leaders develop the company's strategy or vision, which is shared with the other company levels, such as tactical and operational. However, the performance measure systems studied fail to identify and link the organizational performance measures with the other organizational levels using a feedback loop system. Figure 2.4 illustrates the three levels of management and the type of decisions organizations commonly confront.

To identify historical data and measurement tools already in use, the plant manager questionnaire is filled out by the plant manager or operations manager. This step is critical in identifying the key performance measures currently used and the tools utilized to capture the historical data. The plant manager questionnaire developed is included in Appendix B. This questionnaire plays a critical role by identifying the data collection tools, methods, and techniques currently used in the evaluated organization. In addition, this questionnaire helps identify historical data in order to simplify the data collection process and assure the success of the next step. This key step helps to successfully plan the data collection process and anticipate potential problems, such as indicators never measured before.

2.2.3 Data collection: Step 3

Across this book, Pam's manufacturing business will be used to illustrate models and membership functions (MFs) presented in this book. Pam's business focuses on the production of commercial and residential solar panels, and she has manufacturing plants distributed across the United States. While she has over 20 years of experience as a manufacturing leader, she would like to have a tool that can help her make wiser and reliable decisions. Plant A is a subsidiary treated as a cost center. It has 250 full-time employees supporting three shifts. The industry standards are used to develop the quantifiable company success model, and data from Plants A and B are used to validate the developed models. A glossary of terms is provided in order to avoid any misunderstanding with the key performance measures and metrics identified, and to enhance the success and accuracy of the data collection process (see Appendix C).

2.2.4 Model development and membership function mapping of company success components: Step 4

Probability theory has been traditionally used for describing the phenomenon of uncertainty; it deals with the expectation of future events based on something known. However, the uncertainty represented by fuzziness is not the expectation of uncertainty; rather, it is the uncertainty resulting from the imprecision of a concept expressed by a linguistic term. Probability is the theory of random events and the likelihood of events (Klir et al. 1997).

FST is a modeling technique frequently used where vague concepts and imprecise data are handled, and is? capable of managing both imprecision and uncertainty data (Bonissone 1980). FST has been used for the development of the linguistic approach where any variable is treated as a linguistic variable (i.e., low, medium, and high). Linguistic values are created of a syntactic label, a sentence belonging to a term set, and its semantic value. In addition, FST can be used to translate linguistic terms into numeric values. Gilb (1999) suggested following these enumerated steps to develop scales for qualitative data: (1) identify any established scales (perform an extended literature review); (2) check system requirements to identify any scale; (3) ask yourself: what you are trying to alter and how you would measure success; and (4) in the case of dealing with complex variables, break the component into sub concepts until a good level of detail has been achieved. This approach was used in this work to develop a large number of MFs. FST characterizes the concept of approximation based on MFs with a range between 0 and 1, instead including or excluding performance measures. Zimmerman identifies the necessity to use mathematical language to map several MFs and generate FST models.

However, the use of mathematical modeling techniques brings some limitations or challenges. Real situations are not often deterministic or precise, and the description of a real system often requires more detailed data than a human being could ever recognize simultaneously (Schwartz 1962; Zimmermann 1991).

FST provides a good starting point in the development of a conceptual framework and proves to be more useful in the field of pattern classification (Zadeh 1965). In addition, FST provides a framework for dealing with problems in the absence of sharply defined criteria of class membership rather than in the presence or absence of variables. FST provides a rigorous mathematical framework in which vague data can be precisely studied (Zimmermann 1991).

The extensive literature review performed helped in identifying a scale for every company success component and assisted in the development of MFs. In the majority of the cases, an existing scale was not found, leading the MF to be developed based on national averages, industry data, and SMEs.

There are many types of MFs such as linear, triangular, trapezoidal, Gaussian, bell, and sigmoid, but two were selected and applied to develop the MFs described in this book. Linear MFs were selected to characterize the employee morale variables obtained from a survey, and sigmoid MFs were applied to the rest of the company success performance measures.

1. Linear MFs are represented by a straight line and are the simplest type of MF. There are two states of linear fuzzy sets: the increasing state which goes from 0 to 1 degree of membership, and the decreasing state which is the opposite (goes from 1 to 0 degree of membership). This MF is represented in Equation 2.1 by a range and a slope that is characterized by a 45° angle.

$$\Gamma(x) = \begin{cases} 0 \to \chi \le \alpha \\ ((\chi - \alpha)/(\beta - \alpha)) \to \alpha \prec \chi \le \beta \\ 1 \to \chi \succ \beta \end{cases} \tag{2.1}$$

where:
$\alpha = 0$ degree of membership
$\beta = 1$ degree of membership

2. Sigmoid/logistic MFs are also called S-curve MFs and are represented by increasing and decreasing nonlinear functions. A growing sigmoidal MF goes from the left-hand side, which represents no membership, to the extreme right-hand side of the graph, which represents complete membership. Sigmoidal MFs are represented by three parameters: α which represents zero membership value, β the inflection point or the 50% membership point, and γ which represents complete membership value. S-curve MF represents continuous cumulative distribution functions and is commonly used to model population dynamics. Sigmoid MFs are commonly applied in

situations such as average income of executives on the East Coast, mean-time-between-failure (MTBF) of a hard disk drive, or any dynamic value that approximates a continuous random variable (Cox 1994). Equation 2.2 illustrates a Sigmoidal MF.

$$S(x;\alpha,\beta,\gamma) = \begin{cases} 0 \rightarrow \chi \leq \alpha \\ 2((\chi-\alpha)/(\gamma-\alpha))^2 \rightarrow \alpha \leq \chi \leq \beta \\ 1 - 2((\chi-\gamma)/(\gamma-\alpha))^2 \rightarrow \beta \leq \chi \leq \gamma \\ 1 \rightarrow \chi \geq \gamma \end{cases} \tag{2.2}$$

where
   $\alpha = 0$ degree of membership
   $\beta = 0.5$ degree of membership or inflection point
   $\gamma = 1$ degree of membership.

2.2.4.1   Analytical hierarchy process

Hierarchical classifications can help show relationships among categories; this book presents a hierarchical system where taxonomies are developed by organizing data into different levels. To evaluate the feasibility of the categories and ratings, SMEs were asked to review the relative weights obtained through the analytical hierarchy process (AHP). Pairwise comparisons are frequently used to determine the relative importance of each factor variable. Comparisons are made within modules to determine the relationship between the factors identified by the experts. Saaty (1990) developed a rating scale which could be utilized for comparisons where each pair-wise comparison is rated on a scale from 1 to 9. In an AHP analysis, the rating is used to define the degree of preference of one variable over another. The value 1 represents equal importance of the two variables, X and Y, and the value 9 suggests that X is more important than Y. The inverse of the values is used if the expert considers that an inverse relationship exists among the variables. Once the pairwise matrix is developed, the relative weights are obtained from the estimate of the maximum eigenvector of the matrix. The normalized average weighting indicates the relative significance of each factor.

The AHP approach, which consists of a series of goals, criteria, and alternatives, simplifies a complex problem into simple pairwise comparisons. AHP is very useful in complex decision-making, and many softwares are available in the market capable of modeling AHP. Pairwise comparison is a problem-solving method that allows the user to determine the relative order or ranking of a group of items resulting in a specific point value. There is a great variety of software capable of solving

AHP, but Expert Choice was the software selected for this work. The following ratings were used to develop the forms to be sent to all the SMEs (subject matter experts).

1 = X-variable is Equally Important as Y-variable
3 = X-variable is Slightly More Important than Y-variable
−3 = X-variable is Slightly Less Important than Y-variable
5 = X-variable is More Important than Y-variable
−5 = X-variable is Less Important than Y-variable
7 = X-variable is Highly More Important than Y-variable
−7 = X-variable is Highly Less Important than Y-variable
9 = X-variable is Extremely More Important than Y-variable
−9 = X-variable is Extremely Less Important than Y-variable

A pairwise comparison example was included within the form to assist SMEs with the pairwise comparison process and avoid any misunderstanding. Given the scenario that *Profit* and *Productivity* are to be compared, if the SME considers profit to slightly more important than *Productivity*, then the expert should assign 3 to this scenario as shown in Table 2.2.

2.2.4.2   Weights
As discussed in Section 2.2.4.1, a group of SMEs identified the relative importance of company success components and factor variables. This process was performed by comparing each pair of variables or components and ranking them using the following scale: (1, ±3, ±5, ±7, and ±9). An AHP form was created and distributed to all the SMEs.

2.2.4.3   Inconsistency ratio
The inconsistency ratio is used to evaluate the SMEs' ability to make consistent judgments. Basically, this ratio identifies if the SMEs are coherent or forget prior assessments across the exercise. The presence of inconsistency indicates that an SME is not paying attention or that he or she does not understand the assessment tool. Inconsistency ratios smaller than 0.1 reflect a coherent SME; ratios greater than 0.1 represent a concern (Hallowell 2016). A series of pairwise ratio-based comparisons were performed to evaluate SMEs' understanding of company success. This ratio was calculated by evaluating if the whole set of pairwise comparisons was stacking up in a self-consistent way.

Table 2.2 SME sample form

Company Success	Profit	Productivity
Profit	1	3
Productivity	X	1

2.2.4.4   Subject matter experts

SMEs can be used to determine the relative weights of factor variables and assist in the development of FST models. There are different ways to develop MFs that include direct (experts giving answers to various kinds of questions) and indirect methods (ask experts more general and less biased questions, Terano et al. 1992; Klir and Yuan 1995). This approach is beneficial for multifaceted and linguistic variables, and the use of SMEs can assist in the quantification of qualitative performance measures.

Furthermore, research performed by McCauley-Bell and Badiru used knowledge acquisition to obtain factor relevance (McCauley-Bell and Badiru 1996). The scale to develop MFs was developed using the described approach in this research.

2.2.4.5   Company success index model: Step 5

This book presents the combined effects of all the critical success factor variables that affect the overall company success (profit, productivity, efficiency, ergonomics and safety, quality, and employee morale), and an index capable of measuring the relative performance of company success. This model can be benchmarked by other manufacturing organizations and assist others to continuously improve an organization and achieve organizational excellence. The model's mathematical operands were identified by assuming linearity. Since the factors have an accumulating effect, an additive model was developed.

The company success index model is based on a 0–1 scale, where 0–0.33 represents a low level of organizational success, 0.34–0.66 a medium level, and 0.67–1 a high level. Furthermore, this index model is capable of measuring performance across multiple divisions and assisting organizational leaders in the challenging process of multivariable decisions. The combination of MFs and models generates a feasible company success index model that is presented in Chapter 7.

2.2.4.6   Company success index model validation: Step 6

Data obtained from manufacturing plants were used to validate the company success model developed as well as the quality, ergonomics and safety, and employee morale models. Research efforts pursued were directed toward test and verification of the previously described index and methodology. This effort involved testing and verification of the company success index by determining the accuracy of the Fuzzy model.

Several factors must be taken into account in order to design a stable and consistent prediction model. Equation 2.3 is used to calculate accuracy:

$$\text{Accuracy} = TP + TN/(TP + FP + FN + TN) \qquad (2.3)$$

where:
    FP = false-positive
    TN = true-negative
    FN = false-negative
    TP = true-positive

An approach to validate a model is by running the same experiment in a different environment; data collected in different manufacturing plants are used to validate the Fuzzy models developed and presented in the following chapters.

The majority of the MFs presented in this book used national averages and existing scales to map the MFs and identify the degree of membership within the fuzzy set.

2.3 Summary

In conclusion, this chapter presented a new methodology to develop a holistic model to measure organizational success in the manufacturing sector (Ferreras 2008; Ferreras and Crumpton-Young 2013). The described approach can be benchmarked to develop new models using novel methods and techniques that can be used to not only measure and predict any organization, but also to identify areas to improve and obtain the greatest return on investment. The methodology presented in this chapter walks through the process, step by step, describing the tools, methods, and techniques recommended. This chapter includes the rationale behind the selection of the different techniques and approaches to develop the company success index model. It also discusses the steps to develop the MFs and the fuzzy set models to measure company success.

References

Amaratunga, D. and D. Baldry. 2002. Performance measurement in facilities management and its relationships with management theory and motivation. *Facilities,* 20 (10), 327–336.

Banks, R. L. and S. C. Wheelwright 1979. Operations versus Strategy—Trading tomorrow for today. *Harvard Business Review,* 57, 112–20.

Bausch, C. 2015. *Trends Driving the Evolution of the Human Capital Management Industry.* September 1, https://www.linkedin.com/pulse/trends-driving-evolution-human-capital-management-industry-bausch

Bititci, U. S., Carrie, A. S., and L. McDevitt. 1997. Integrated performance measurement systems: A development guide. *International Journal of Operations and Production Management,* 17, 522–534.

Bititci, U., Mendibil, K., Martinez, V., and P. Albores. 2005. Measuring and managing performance in extended enterprises. *International Journal of Operations & Production Management,* 25, 333–353.

Bonissone, P. P. 1980. A fuzzy sets based linguistic approach: Theory and applications. *Proceedings of the 1980 Winter Simulation Conference.* Orlando, FL, pp. 99–111.

Bourne, M., Mills, J. Wilcox, M. Neely, A., and K. Platts. 2000. Designing, implementing and updating performance measurement systems. *International Journal of Operations & Production Management*, 20(7), 754–771.

Bourque, P., Stroian, V., and A. Abran. 2006. Proposed concepts for a tool for multidimensional performance modeling in software engineering management. *IEEE ISIE*, July 9–12, Montreal, Quebec, Canada. http://www.gelog.etsmtl.ca/publications/pdf/1014.pdf

Busi, M. and U. Bititci. 2006. Collaborative performance management: Present gaps and future research. *International Journal of Productivity and Performance Management*, 55 (1), 7–25.

Cox, E. 1994. *The Fuzzy Systems Handbook: A Practitioner's Guide to Building, Using, and Maintaining Fuzzy Systems*. San Diego, CA: Academic Press, Inc.

Cross, K. F. and R. L. Lynch. 1989. The SMART way to define and sustain success. *National Productivity Review*, 8, 23–33.

Devitt, J. 2001. *Joseph Stiglitz Wins Nobel Prize for Economics: Third Economist to Win Prize in Six Years*. Columbia News, City of New York. http://www.columbia.edu/cu/news/01/10/josephStiglitz_nobel_2001.html

Dixon J., Nanni R., Alfred J. Jr., and T. E. Vollmann. 1990. *The New Performance Challenge: Measuring Operations for World-Class Competition*. Homewood, IL: Business One Irwin.

Evans, J. R. and W. M. Lindsay. 2002. *The Management and Control of Quality*, 5th edition. Cincinnati, OH: South-Western, Thompson Learning, pp. 115, 462.

Ferreras, A. 2008. A comprehensive multi-faceted approach for simultaneously analyzing organizational performance measures essential for company success in manufacturing enterprises. *ProQuest LLC*, pp. 1–214.

Ferreras, A. and L. Crumpton-Young. 2013. The measure of success. *Industrial Management*, May/June, 26–30.

Frängsmyr, T. 2004. *The Sveriges Riksbank Prize in Economic Sciences in Memory of Alfred Nobel 2003*. Les Prix Nobel. The Nobel Prizes 2003, Nobel Foundation. http://nobelprize.org/nobel_prizes/economics/laureates/2003/engle-autobio.html

Frigo, M. L. and K. R. Krumwiede. 1999. Balanced scorecards: A rising trend in strategic performance measurement. *Journal of Strategic Performance Measurement*, 3, 42–48.

Garengo, P., Biazzo, S., and U. S. Bititci. 2005. Performance measurement systems in SMEs: A review for a research agenda. *International Journal of Management Reviews*, 7 (1), 25–47. May 3.

Ghalayini, A. and J. Noble. 1996. The changing basis of performance measurement. *International Journal of Operations & Production Management*, 16 (8), 63–80.

Gilb, T. 1999. Advanced requirements specification: Quantifying the qualitative. *PSQT Conference*, St. Paul MN, October 5, pp. 1–8.

Globerson S. 1985. *Performance Criteria and Incentive Systems*. Elsevier Publishing, Amsterdam.

Guru99. 2016. Accessed December 1, 2016. http://www.guru99.com/mis-definition.html

Hallowell, D. 2016. *Analytical Hierarchy Process (AHP)—Getting Oriented*. iSixSigma LLC. Accessed November 22, 2016. https://www.isixsigma.com/tools-templates/analytic-hierarchy-process-ahp/analytical-hierarchy-process-ahp-%E2%90%93-getting-oriented/

Hayes, R. H. and D. A. Garvin. 1982. Managing as if tomorrow mattered. *Harvard Business Review*, May–June, 70–79.

Institute of Management Accountants. 1998. *Tools and Techniques for Implementing Integrated Performance Management Systems*. Montvale, NJ: Institute of Management Accountants.

Kaplan, R. S. and D. P. Norton. 1992. The balanced scorecard: Measures that drive performance. *Harvard Business Review*, January–February, 71–79.

Kaplan, R. S. and D. P. Norton. 1996. *The Balanced Scorecard: Translating Strategy into Action*. Boston: Harvard Business School Press.

Kaplan, R. S. and D. P. Norton. 2002. Partnering and the balanced scorecard. *HBS Working Knowledge Newsletter*. http://hbswk.hbs.edu/item/3231.html

Klir, G. J., St. Clair, U. H., and B. Yuan. 1997. *Fuzzy Set Theory: Foundations and Applications*. Upper Saddle River, NJ: Prentice-Hall.

Klir, G. J. and B. Yuan. 1995. *Fuzzy Sets and Fuzzy Logic: Theory and Applications*. Upper Saddle, NJ: Prentice-Hall.

Lynch, R. L. and K. F. Cross. 1991. *Measure Up! Yardsticks for Continuous Improvement*. Cambridge, MA: Basil Blackwell.

McCauley-Bell, P. and A. Badiru. 1996. Fuzzy modeling and analytic hierarch processing—Means to quantify risk levels associated with occupational injuries—Part I: The development of a fuzzy linguistic risk levels. *IEEE Transactions on Fuzzy Systems*, 4 (2), 121–134.

Neely A., Gregory M., and K. Platts. 2005. Performance measurement system design: A literature review and research agenda. *International Journal of Operations & Production Management*, 25 (12), 1228–1263.

Pollalis Y. and I. Koliousis. 2003. Enterprise performance measurement: Using the balanced scorecard for business optimization. *Journal of Applied Systems Studies*, 4 (3), 7.

Rolstadas, A. 1998. Enterprise performance measurement. *International Journal of Operations & Production Management*, 18, 989–999, MCB University Press.

Saaty, T. L. 1990. How to make a decision: The analytic hierarchy process. *European Journal of Operational Research*, 48 (1), 9–26.

Schwartz, J. 1962. The pernicious influence of mathematics in science. In: Nagel, Supper, and Tarski. *Logic Methodology and Philosophy of Science*. Stanford, CA.

Sink, D. S. 1985. *Productivity Management: Planning, Measurement and Evaluation, Control and Improvement*. New York: John Wiley & Sons.

Sink, D. S. and T. C. Tuttle. 1989. *Planning and Measurement in Your Organization of the Future*. Norcross, GA: Industrial Engineering and Management Press.

Sink, D. S. and T. C. Tuttle. January/February 1990. The performance management question in the organization of the future. *Industrial Management*, 32 (1), 4–12.

Terano T., Asai K., and M. Sugeno. 1992. *Fuzzy Systems Theory and Its Applications*. San Diego, CA: Academic Press, Inc.

Truccolo, I., Bianchet, K., Ciolfi, L., Michilin, N., Giacomello, E., Parro, A., Ricci, R., Flego, A., and P. De Paoli. 2005. EFQM and libraries: An organizational challenge for improving the provided services. EAHIL Workshop. *Implementation of Quality Systems and Certification of Biomedical Libraries*, Palermo, June 23–25.

Zadeh, L. A. 1965. Fuzzy sets. *Information and Control*, 8, 338–353.

Zimmermann, H.-J. 1991. *Fuzzy Set Theory and Its Applications*, 2nd edition. Dordrecht: Kluwer Academic Publisher.

chapter three

Employee morale
The Ferreras model

There are many definitions of employee morale, which can be classified into two types. The first type assigns the responsibility to the employer, such as Dr. David Javitch (2005) who defines it as the end result of many factors present in the workplace environment. The second type puts the focus on the employee, and that is the case with Nicole Fink who defines employee morale as the human behavior of individuals (i.e., happiness, engagement, etc.) employed by an organization (Blankenship 2014).

Company leaders often think that just paying a salary to an employee for performing a job or a series of tasks is good enough. In their minds, wages and some benefits should be enough to make employees give their best and advance the business. Employees typically expect much more than a salary from their employers, such as rewards, involvement in key decisions, appreciation, etc. Investing in employee morale is often perceived by company leaders more like an option than a requirement. They overlook that employees can transform a company into a market leader or can also end a business. Employee morale has been proven to have an impact on all other key components of company success, such as profit, productivity, efficiency, quality, and ergonomics and safety. Therefore, it should be a business priority for all organizations to measure employee morale and make improvements. Gallup reports that companies with highly satisfied groups of employees often exhibit above-average levels of the following characteristics (Corporate Leadership Council 2003):

- Customer loyalty (56%)
- Productivity (50%)
- Employee retention (50%)
- Safety records (50%)
- Profitability (33%)

Gallup estimates that there are 22 million actively disengaged employees costing the American economy as much as $350 billion per year in lost productivity including absenteeism, illness, and other problems that result when employees are unhappy at work. According to the CCH Unscheduled Absence Survey, employers have failed to make significant improvement against the costly absenteeism problem that takes billions of dollars off the bottom line for U.S. businesses. The nation's largest employers estimate that unscheduled absenteeism costs their businesses more than $760,000 per year in direct payroll costs, and even more when lower productivity, lost revenue, and the effects of poor morale are considered (Blankenship 2014).

Dissatisfied employees make more mistakes, take longer to get tasks done, report more sick days, leave their jobs more often, and profit decreases. Most importantly, companies with low employee morale do not lead markets. Mark Crowley describes in "How SAS Became the World's Best Place to Work" how SAS's CEO, Jim Goodnight has built a company with only a 2%–3% turnover rate, instead of the 22% industry average. According to Forbes, Goodnight is now the 47th richest man in America, with an estimated net worth of $7.3 billion and has led SAS to 37 consecutive years of record earnings by setting employee morale as the business priority (Crowley 2013).

We have all worked for a company with low employee morale at some point in our lives since that is the norm more than the exception. While the experience can vary, it always affects employees' performance in a negative way. Employees with low morale not only make more mistakes, but also they get involved in more accidents in the workplace. Although a company leader might be investing in quality and safety to reduce the number of defects and accidents, low employee morale could be causing it and preventing the company from becoming successful. The leaders of a company with low morale clearly have developed a poor workplace environment and often lose their greatest asset, the best employees. Good corporate leaders truly care about their human capital; they evaluate the situation and want to hear what their employees have to say about their engagement and the workplace environment. However, company leaders always want to hire the best human capital but fail to retain them. If a leader is that person whom you will follow to a place where you will never dare to go alone, the ability of leaders to retain their employees is key to lead a successful business. To keep the best employees, organizational leaders must continue investing in them and always aim to improve the workplace environment. In many organizations, leaders don't embrace the importance of investing in efforts to increase employee morale and thus morale of the employees suffers.

The Ferreras theory is introduced in this chapter. This new employee morale theory consists of controllable and uncontrollable forces. While the employer has control over the policies or conditions that affect the workplace environment, it is impossible to engage everyone. However, it is only by caring to know what the situation is and having the ultimate desire to have happy employees that a leader can bring a company to the top. Customers are always looking for better customer service, and QSR magazine online suggests that happier, more accountable employees naturally improve customer service. There is a direct relationship between employee satisfaction and customer satisfaction (Colburn 2015).

This chapter reviews the importance of employee morale and the key role it plays in the success of manufacturing organizations. This chapter also presents a new theory and model to measure employee morale success and the improvement areas with a greater return on investment. Managers in human resource (HR) departments and business leaders can easily use the model to make wiser decisions regarding their employees. This approach not only allows the user to know what is important for the employees, but also where it makes more sense to invest in order to improve the employee morale.

3.1   The evolution of employee morale: Theories and perspectives

Abraham (1943) published a paper titled "a theory of human motivation" in *Psychological Review* where he introduces the hierarchy of needs. Maslow used the terms *physiological, safety, belongingness, and love, esteem, self-actualization, and self-transcendence* to describe the pattern that human motivations generally move through. Figure 3.1 illustrates some of Maslow's theory with additional variables that describe the needs that humans have for recognition, rewards, and appreciation.

Frederick Herzberg discovered during the 1950s and 1960s that motivation, as it pertains to improved job performance, was directly related to the upper two levels of Maslow's hierarchy, *esteem and self-actualization* needs. Herzberg stated that, in the workplace, *esteem and self-actualization* are satisfied by the nature of the work itself and the drive to satisfy these needs results in more mature and productive behaviors. Herzberg called these upper-level needs *motivators,* and individuals interested in obtaining these needs come into an organization having their lower-level needs met

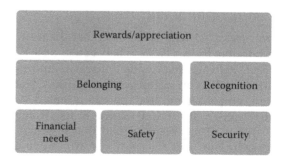

Figure 3.1 Some Maslow variables.

and expecting challenges and opportunity from their work. Sometimes, individuals have a high tolerance for poorer *hygiene factors* such as basic *security and social* needs if the *motivators* such as *esteem and self-actualization* needs are present. Herzberg called *maintenance seekers* employees who are particularly preoccupied with *hygiene factors. Maintenance seekers* are people who may have been denied satisfaction of lower-level needs in the past and have spent most of their lives struggling to have those needs met. Sometimes, *maintenance seekers* are happy to have a good paying job and safe amenable working conditions, and do not have a strong drive to grow or be given higher responsibilities.

The Great Place to Work® began in 1981 when two business journalists, Robert Levering and Milton Moskowitz published a book titled *The 100 Best Companies to Work for in America*. Levering and Moskowitz consider key to create a great workplace that builds high-quality relationships in the workplace, such as *trust, pride, and camaraderie*. The Great Place to Work assisted the Fortune family to develop The Best Companies to Work For® list, which has become a popular index used worldwide to rank companies based on employee morale. The Great Place to Work developed the Trust Index© Employee Survey, which is the primary tool for assessing and rating organizations that appear on the annual Fortune 100 Best Companies to Work For list. Companies nominated for Best Companies to Work For lists must go through an application process to get selected and ranked. Two-thirds of the score come from the Trust Index Survey, which measures employee perception of the workplace. The other one-third of the total score comes from the Culture Audit©, which is completed by management and evaluated by an independent Great Place to Work team. Two-thirds of a company's workplace culture assessment is based on the employee survey; one-third is based on the company's policies and practices, as measured in the Culture Audit.

3.2   *Understanding your employees and your organizational culture*

The textbook *Principles of Management* states that the term organizational culture became popular in the 1980s when Peters and Waterman's best-selling book *In Search of Excellence* made the argument that company success could be attributed to an organizational culture that was decisive, customer-oriented, empowering, and people-oriented (Carpenter et al. 2009). An organization's culture may be one of its strongest assets or its biggest liability. In fact, it has been argued that organizations that have a rare and hard-to-imitate culture enjoy a competitive advantage. In a survey conducted by the management consulting firm Bain & Company in 2007, worldwide business leaders identified *corporate culture* to be as important as *corporate strategy* for business success (Barney 1986). This comes as no surprise to leaders of successful businesses, who are quick to attribute their company's success to their organization's culture (HR Focus 2007).

Every company has its own organizational culture, and it is important to understand the culture before you can make any major change. Employee morale might vary greatly among manufacturing plants, sites, or subsidiaries within the same company due to different cultures and leaders, among other factors. Therefore, it is key to understand the organizational culture in every site before making any major decision on human capital. HR departments focus on the employees and their well-being, from hiring to terminations, and their managers along with the company leaders play a key role in shaping up the workplace environment and employee engagement. Two manufacturing plants producing the same goods for the same company in different locations can easily have different cultures and employee morale levels since their workplace environments, policies, employees, and leaders will vary. Understanding the culture in every site is a must before making standardized employee morale decisions across the entire institution.

3.3 Internal and external factors in employee morale

Employee Morale is affected by internal and external factors. External factors are uncontrollable, such as market change, economic recessions, political changes, and disrupted technologies, just to mention some. While they are uncontrollable by nature, good business leaders know how to navigate through them and minimize the negative effects on their employees. For example, economic recessions often lead customers to spend less; and in manufacturing businesses lower sales lead to less production. In those cases, most business leaders reduce their workforce, which has serious implications for employee morale. While common manufacturing leaders retain their best employees and perform layoffs, top business leaders who achieve high employee morale do not.

James Goodnight, CEO of SAS, a software company that has grown since it was established in 1981, has successfully navigated five recessions. At the end of October 2008, new sales revenues were up 12.5%, but things changed in November and December when it stopped. SAS ended the year with a gain of 5.1%. Everyone else was laying people off, so SAS employees were really concerned. In January 2009, James made it very clear that he was not going to lay off anyone. He just asked everyone to reduce expenses. In the end, revenue rose about 2.2% and expenses went up less than 1% so James was pleased. Often, leaders do not realize the implications layoffs have on employee morale. A Stanford professor wrote an article about how SAS benefits affect retention. He estimated that SAS saves between $60 million and $80 million a year not having to replace people. SAS's turnover has seldom exceeded 4% a year, and a lot of that is retirement (Buchanan 2011).

Internal factors in employee morale are those that can be easily controlled by the organizational leaders; for example, management style, organizational culture, and workplace environment, among others. One of the most common internal factors that are not mastered by many company leaders is communication. David Hassell, a serial entrepreneur and CEO, states that open communication is vital to business success. Almost all company leaders claim to value it, but few truly achieve it (Hassell 2014). Relationships are built up through continued open and honest communication. When employees do not feel comfortable approaching a supervisor, either with ideas or problems, management runs the risk of not getting the best from the human capital. In other words, they are not optimizing the employees' potential. Employees should be encouraged to voice their ideas and concerns to management without repercussions, and a mechanism should be in place to ensure that it is practiced (Morgan 2015).

3.4   Human capital in manufacturing organizations

Shawn Grimsley states that human capital is the sum total of a person's knowledge, skills, and energy that the company can use to become successful. Human capital is the most valuable intangible asset a leader can have to bring a company to its fullest potential. While money and other resources cannot stretch, workers can go beyond leaders' desires and expectations. Top companies nurture their employees, involve them, and empower them to a point where workers generate innovative ideas and solutions that go beyond their job description and boss's expectations (Grimsley 2015).

HR managers and company leaders are involved in acquiring, cultivating, and retaining the best human capital. As much as advances in technology allow us to design better machines capable of handling systemized processes that require less employees, human capital continues to be one of the greatest assets a manufacturing company can have. In fact, top performing company leaders know that being able to attract the best human capital in their sector is what sets them apart from the rest of the competitors. We live in a knowledge-based economy, and highly skilled human capital brings a collection of resources, such as knowledge, creativity, talents, skills, abilities, experience, intelligence, training, judgment, and wisdom, that produce a great economic value for any business. These resources are the total capacity of the people that represents a form of wealth which can be directed to become the market leader in any sector. Manufacturing businesses have white collar and blue collar positions, and the workforce varies among these employees. It is important to remember, however, that individuals are only assets to the degree company leaders invest in their human capital. While employees bring competencies, experiences, and attributes to an enterprise, their commitment to bring the company to the top must be there to optimize their contribution. This then throws the spotlight on how businesses invest in their human capital asset, in order for it to add value. This is an important component for manufacturing leaders to understand so that they can make optimal decisions. Understanding how people add value to an organization and being able to monitor it and invest in it, it is an important advantage that HR managers and corporate leaders in the twenty-first century should tap into (IThound 2007).

3.5 The evolution of decision-making on human capital and employee morale

Organizations such as IBM were among the first to measure, understand, and gain insight into workplace concepts like morale, employees' satisfaction, and commitment. It has been an evolution from a focus on *job satisfaction* in the 1970s to a focus on *commitment* in the 1980s and 1990s, and a focus on *employee engagement* from the year 2000 to the present (Van Rooy and Oehler 2013).

Numerous studies support that there is a link between employee satisfaction and customer satisfaction, productivity, and financial results (Corporate Leadership Council 2003). Company leaders are finally realizing that the field of human resources (HRs) and the management of human capital have become more relevant to bring a company to the top and compete in the current competitive market. Therefore, the ability to have data and make non biased workforce decisions is a significant advantage.

Nowadays, leading organizations are using more rigorous and reliable statistical techniques with their business data. Relative Weight Analysis and Structural Equation Modeling are commonly used by those designing surveys for employees. Also, performance measures and metrics are more commonly used nowadays. Company leaders are increasingly using data-driven approaches to provide the greatest degree of confidence behind prioritization activities that are derived from employee surveys (Van Rooy and Oehler 2013).

The workplace continues to evolve at an escalating pace. Some reports are predicting further globalization of business, increased mobility both for the worker and in the workplace, and more cultural integration on social and corporate levels. Workforce planning requires more attention than ever. Having a system to measure and evaluate employee morale can help companies be able to better determine hiring needs with their budgets and look into workforce trends to predict future success. Despite the evolution and uncertainty, trends are arising that give new opportunity for HR leaders to get more involved in business decisions (Arash 2014).

3.6 Business ethics

Just like every company has an organizational culture, every business has its own ethics, which is an intrinsic part of its culture. A company with poor business ethics can't earn employees' full trust and respect. It is impossible to expect employees to be engaged in a business with poor ethics and values. Therefore, it is critically important to set HR practices that entail good values, ethics, and fairness. When it comes to business ethics, there is nothing better than to lead by example.

3.6.1 Accountability

Organizational structures help leaders to have a clear understanding of who does what, and who is accountable for specific job responsibilities and decisions. It is important that employees feel accountable and empowered to make decisions and bring the company to the top. To achieve that, leaders must empower their employees and provide them enough information and resources to make optimal decisions. Often, leaders do not share enough information with their employees, which jeopardizes their ability to make good decisions. Absenteeism represents a poor sense of accountability in any organization, and generates a great loss.

3.6.2 Transparency

In the past decade, there has been a movement on transparency that has affected all types of organizations. When folks talk about transparency, they tend to mean financial transparency. However, employees want HR processes and practices to be more transparent as well. Discrimination may occur in American organizations and those businesses that do not demonstrate having in place transparent hiring processes, promotions, and the ultimate goal of hiring a diverse group of employees suffer. Many leaders justify the lack of diversity due to the lack of qualified candidates from underrepresented minority groups. Those leaders do not understand that placing their buddies or friends in management and leadership positions will hurt more than help their businesses. Workforce diversity is key to obtaining best outcomes in every single level of an organization. Products designed by employees with different backgrounds, race, and skill-set are more robust and have a greater probability of satisfying a broader spectrum of customers.

3.7 The Ferreras theory: A holistic approach to evaluate and measure employee morale

While the 100 Best Companies to Work for list provides a criterion to measure employee morale, it only takes into account several performance measures, such as trust, fairness, respect, pride, camaraderie, and credibility (TRC 2012). Instead, using a limited perspective, the Ferreras theory provides a more holistic and multifaceted approach for measuring, evaluating, and predicting employee morale. The following pyramid illustrates the Ferreras theory and the two subcomponents that resonate with the Maslow and Herzberg theories. The Ferreras theory states that employee morale relies upon a set of controllable factors that fall under *workplace environment* and a set of uncontrollable factors that fall under *employee engagement*. While many HR managers and corporate leaders are focusing on increasing employee engagement, it is impossible to think that all employees can be engaged. Figure 3.2 illustrates the comparison between the Maslow and Herzberg theories.

This theory considers that every organization has a series of controllable factor variables, which are based on the *work environment* created by the organization, and a series of uncontrollable factor variables based on the *employee engagement*, which will vary among employees. The Ferreras theory is similar to the Herzberg theory in the sense that Ferreras *employee engagement* factor variables would be Herzberg's *motivators* and Ferreras *work environment* factor variables would be Herzberg's *hygiene factors*. However, the Ferreras theory takes a greater variety of factor variables into account to have a more holistic and multifaceted approach to characterize, measure, and predict employee morale. Figure 3.3 shows the employee morale taxonomy, the subcomponents, as well as the key performance measures essential for a successful manufacturing business. The Ferreras

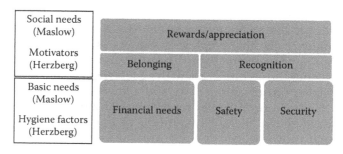

Figure 3.2 Maslow and Herzberg theories.

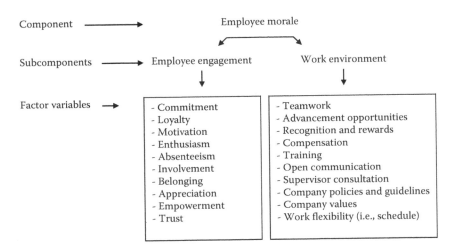

Figure 3.3 *Employee Morale* taxonomy.

theory is based on factor variables or key performance measures that have been identified in the literature review and SMEs' opinion. Figure 3.3 illustrates the Employee Morale taxonomy or categorization structure.

3.7.1   Employee engagement

Employee engagement represents those variables that are uncontrollable by the employer. In other words, an employer might want to increase employee involvement, but at the end of the day, employees might or might not get involved. While certain practices might get some employees involved, others might need different approaches. Unless employees are engaged, the employer's efforts might be a waste. Herzberg called these factor variables *motivators,* and just like not all human beings are motivated by the same things, not all the employees are engaged the same way.

According to Kerry Butters, studies show that engaged employees work harder, are often willing to take on extra responsibilities, and are a positive influence on other employees. Butters says that employees who are actively disengaged tend to be disruptive and a bad influence on others. However, for those companies with a high engagement level, benefits include a higher rate of productivity and a lower staff turnover (Butters 2013). Dov Seidman from Forbes reported in 2012 that a Towers Watson survey indicated that nearly two-thirds of employees in the United States are not fully engaged in their work and are less productive as a result (Seidman 2012). According to Tim Rutledge's publication *Getting Engaged: The New Workplace Loyalty,* employees who are truly engaged are inspired, committed, love their job, and care about the company's future. Companies have to work harder nowadays to gain and retain top talent (Butters 2013). In 2012, a Gallup study of 23,910 business units compared top quartile and bottom quartile engagement scores and found that those in the top quartile averaged a 12% higher profitability (Gallup 2012). Specialists at the Conference Board calculated that over half the U.S. population hates their job. Gallup states that fewer than 3 in 10 workers admit having their hearts in their jobs. Crowley stated that in 2013 alone, the lack of employee engagement was going to cost business upward of $300 billion (Crowley 2013).

The following factors represent *employee engagement* in the Ferreras' theory, and their definitions within the context of a company are

- The sense of *belonging* is developed when a human feels identified by a group or topic, such as an organization or an organization's workforce. Belongingness is the human emotional need to be an accepted member of a group. Since not everyone has the same life and interests, not everyone belongs to the same group or organization, also defined as the quality or state of being an essential or important part of something (Dictionary.com 2015).
- *Involvement* is to affect the scope of an initiative or take the action of participating in a group. While many employees do their work, they do not necessarily get involved in activities or initiatives their employers organize or offer. Employee involvement also includes the ability of a company's management and leadership to involve employees before making decisions related to their jobs or tasks.
- *Enthusiasm* is the feeling of excitement, lively interest, or eagerness. Employees are enthusiastic about their jobs when they find them interesting and fulfilling. In other words, they feel like contributors to the success of the enterprise (Dictionary.com 2015).
- *Motivation* is having a reason or energy to act or accomplish something. It is a personal stimulus that makes human beings achieve or accomplish desired tasks (Dictionary.com 2015).
- *Commitment* is a pledge, promise, or obligation. It is a sense of responsibility that makes human beings feel determined and be persistent. Committed employees are those devoted to the work tasks assigned (Dictionary.com 2015).
- *Loyalty* is faithful adherence to a leader, company, or cause. Loyal employees are proud workers who envision their future associated with an organization. It is what makes human beings come back, just like faithful customers return to buy from the same seller, even though other options exist in the market (Dictionary.com 2015).
- *Trust* is the reliance on the integrity, strength, and ability of a leader or company. It is the confidence human beings can develop and the

hardest factor to attain in employee morale (Dictionary.com 2015). Employees trust their employers when they observe high ethics and integrity in the organization and its management and leadership. David Williams states in Forbes that trust is the most valuable business commodity (Williams 2013). A Fortune 100 Best Places to Work study shows that companies with higher employee trust are more profitable (World Economic Forum and PwC 2015).

- *Appreciation* is gratitude. It is a thankful recognition, acknowledgment, or reward. Appreciation also entails when a manager listens to the suggestions of their employees and thanks them for the extra effort.
- *Empowerment* is to be motivated to work and act upon a task or a cause. The World Bank defines it as the process of increasing the capacity of individuals or groups to make choices and to transform those choices into desired actions and outcomes (World Bank 2011).
- *Absenteeism* is the frequency or habit of not showing up to work. Absenteeism costs U.S. companies billions of dollars each year in lost productivity, wages, poor quality of goods/services, and excess management time. Just in manufacturing, the annual cost of lost productivity due to absenteeism is $2.8B (Folger 2015).
- *Turnover* is when employees are hired to replace those who left or were fired during a 12-month period (Business Dictionary 2015). An analysis of data from PwC Saratoga and the International Labor Organization suggests that for a U.S. company with 10,000 employees, this level of annual turnover would mean a loss of $7.3 million in recruitment fees alone. The Hays Group estimates that global levels of staff turnover are currently running at an average of around 22% per year (World Economic Forum and PwC 2015).

3.7.2 Work environment

As mentioned earlier, work environment represents those variables that are controllable by the employer. If an employer wants to increase employees' rewards or salaries, the company leaders can make that change.

Herzberg called these factor variables *hygiene factors*, and those looking for them are maintenance seekers. The following factors represent *work environment* in the Ferreras' theory, and their definitions within the context of a company are

- *Open communication* is the business environment where the information flows among employees (Manker 2015). Often, company's leadership and management do not openly share enough information with their employees, which affects the ability of employees to make wise decisions and perform their job tasks. Communication in a business can be effective, ineffective, positive, and negative, among the most common types observed. It is important to have positive and effective communication, but openness is key for data sharing.

- *Recognition and rewards* are provided by thankful employers and leaders who appreciate the work, contributions, and commitment of their employees. The human capital of a business often gets rewarded for its performance and for striving to achieve excellence.
- *Advancement opportunities* are the chance an enterprise provides to its employees for growth and advance in their careers within the organization. They are provided by employers who want their human capital to grow and who envision keeping them in the long term. The lack of this factor has an impact on employee retention and other employee morale variables.
- *Teamwork* is the group of coworkers that together achieves goals and tasks. Unifying forces help humans achieve major accomplishments that by themselves could not be achieved. High performing teams are a key asset for business leaders.
- *Compensation* is the wages paid to an employee for performing a task or job.
- *Training* is the professional development opportunities offered by an organization to its employees.
- *Supervisory consultation* is when an employee feels comfortable talking to his/her supervisor whenever there is a problem or an important decision needs to be made.
- *Company policies and guidelines* are the set of rules stipulated by a business for employees to carry on the work. Policies and operating procedures should be fair and explained adequately to all the employees. These are supposed to be equally applied without any favoritism.
- *Company values* are the ethics a business exemplifies, such as honesty, integrity, and fairness, among others.
- *Work flexibility* is the freedom or room that a job offers to an employee. That might entail work schedule, vacation dates, teleworking, etc. Butters states that flexibility in the workplace is important since it increases the morale, as studies prove that it produces less absenteeism, higher engagement and productivity. She also claims that those employees who are given the opportunity for flexible work feel much more trusted and valued than those who do not (Butters 2013).

3.8 The Ferreras model: A holistic approach

The Ferreras model provides a mechanism to evaluate and measure the employee morale using a holistic and multifaceted approach. Company leaders can see how specific employee morale factors affect their business and compare their organizations with industry averages and other competitors. The employee morale model is proposed to holistically characterize the human capital area per site or manufacturing plant annually, considering two subcomponents: employee engagement and work environment. The following equation illustrates the employee morale fuzzy model.

$$EM\,(Plan,\,Year) = WE + EE \tag{3.1}$$

where:
  EM = the "employee morale" component
  WE = the "work environment" subcomponent
  EE = the "employee engagement" subcomponent

To obtain the identified employee morale subcomponents, the following equations illustrate the subcomponents equations:

$$\begin{aligned} WE\,(Plant,\,Year) = {} & (W_1 \times X_1) + (W_2 \times X_2) + (W_3 \times X_3) + (W_4 \times X_4) \\ & + (W_5 \times X_5) + (W_6 \times X_6) + (W_7 \times X_7) + (W_8 \times X_8) \\ & + (W_9 \times X_9) + (W_{10} \times X_{10}) \end{aligned} \tag{3.2}$$

where:
  WE represents the "work environment" subcomponent
  W_1 represents the weight of "open communication"
  X_1 is the level of "open line of communication with management"
  W_2 represents the weight of "recognition & rewards"
  X_2 is the level of "recognition & rewards by management"
  W_3 represents the weight of "advancement opportunities"
  X_3 is the level of "advancement opportunities"
  W_4 represents the weight of "teamwork"
  X_4 is the level of "teamwork"
  W_5 represents the weight of "compensation"
  X_5 is the level of "compensation"
  W_6 represents the weight of "training"
  X_6 is the level of "training opportunities"
  W_7 represents the weight of "supervisory consultation"
  X_7 is the level of "comfortable consulting employee's supervisor"
  W_8 represents the weight of "company policies and guidelines"
  X_8 is the level of "fair company policies and guidelines"
  W_9 represents the weight of "company values"

X_9 is the level of "better company values within an organization"
W_{10} represents the weight of "work flexibility"
X_{10} is the level of "more work flexibility"

$$EE\,(Plant,\,Year) = (W_{11} \times X_{11}) + (W_{12} \times X_{12}) + (W_{13} \times X_{13}) + (W_{14} \times X_{14})$$
$$+ (W_{15} \times X_{15}) + (W_{16} \times X_{16}) + (W_{17} \times X_{17}) + (W_{18} \times X_{18})$$
$$+ (W_{19} \times X_{19}) + (W_{20} \times X_{20}) + (W_{21} \times X_{21}) \qquad (3.3)$$

where:
  EE represents the "employee engagement" subcomponent
  W_{11} represents the weight of "belonging"
  X_{11} is the level of "belonging to a work team/work family"
  W_{12} represents the weight of "involving"
  X_{12} is the level of "involvement in decision-making and company activities"
  W_{13} represents the weight of "enthusiasm"
  X_{13} is the level of "enthusiastic about your job"
  W_{14} represents the weight of "motivation"
  X_{14} is the level of "motivation"
  W_{15} represents the weight of "commitment"
  X_{15} is the level of "commitment and devotion to work"
  W_{16} represents the weight of "loyalty"
  X_{16} is the level of "loyal to the organization"
  W_{17} represents the weight of "trust"
  X_{17} is the level of "trust in management"
  W_{18} represents the weight of "appreciation"
  X_{18} is the level of "appreciation by supervisor"
  W_{19} represents the weight of "empowerment"
  X_{19} is the level of "empowerment to make own decisions"
  W_{20} represents the weight of "absenteeism"
  X_{20} is the percentage of "absenteeism"
  W_{21} represents the weight of "turnover"
  X_{21} is the percentage of "turnover"

3.9 Weights

As mentioned in Chapter 2, weights are obtained from SMEs after performing a pairwise comparison as part of using the Analytical Hierarchy Process technique. While many software choices are available, Expert Choice was used to calculate the employee morale weights. Figure 3.4 illustrates the employee morale weights.

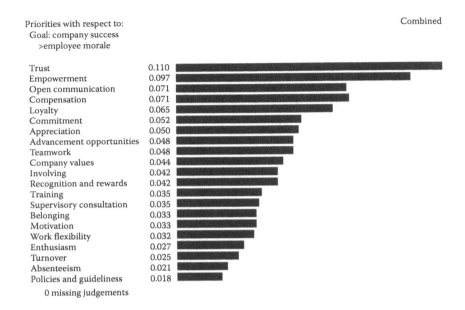

Priorities with respect to:　　　　　　　　　　　　　　　　　　Combined
Goal: company success
　>employee morale

Trust	0.110
Empowerment	0.097
Open communication	0.071
Compensation	0.071
Loyalty	0.065
Commitment	0.052
Appreciation	0.050
Advancement opportunities	0.048
Teamwork	0.048
Company values	0.044
Involving	0.042
Recognition and rewards	0.042
Training	0.035
Supervisory consultation	0.035
Belonging	0.033
Motivation	0.033
Work flexibility	0.032
Enthusiasm	0.027
Turnover	0.025
Absenteeism	0.021
Policies and guideliness	0.018

0 missing judgements

Figure 3.4 Employee morale index model weights.

3.10　Employee morale survey

The purpose of this survey is to estimate quantitatively the employee morale factor variables with qualitative measures, such as motivation level, using a 1–4 scale in combination with the Contingent Valuation technique which helps in prioritizing employee morale decisions using a return on investment approach. The Contingent Valuation technique uses the "willingness to pay" (WTP) concept to assign a value to an intangible or qualitative performance measure. This is a sophisticated cost-benefit measurement approach that assigns a financial value to intangible costs and benefits, such as employee motivation. The employee morale survey measures and evaluates the Ferreras theory variables represented in Figure 3.4. The following list represents the prerequisites for survey participants:

- Males and females
- Over the age of 18
- Workers from any department within the organization
- Full-time employees with a minimum of 6 months seniority (to make sure survey participants have been exposed to the workplace environment)

Table 3.1 shows the component, subcomponents, performance measures, and metrics to be used for data collection of employee morale.

Table 3.1 Employee morale characterization with metrics or taxonomy

Component	Subcomponents	Performance measures	Metrics
Employee morale	Employee engagement	Commitment	1–4 Employee morale scale
		Loyalty	1–4 Employee morale scale
		Motivation	1–4 Employee morale scale
		Enthusiasm	1–4 Employee morale scale
		Absenteeism	Absenteeism rate
		Involving	1–4 Employee morale scale
		Belonging	1–4 Employee morale scale
		Appreciation	1–4 Employee morale scale
		Empowerment	1–4 Employee morale scale
		Trust	1–4 Employee morale scale
		Turnover	Turnover rate
	Work environment	Teamwork	1–4 Employee morale scale
		Advancement opportunities/promotions	1–4 Employee morale scale
		Recognition and rewards	1–4 Employee morale scale
		Compensation	1–4 Employee morale scale
		Training	1–4 Employee morale scale
		Open communication (leave office door open)	1–4 Employee morale scale
		Supervisor consultation (advising, counseling, coaching, mentoring, and listening)	1–4 Employee morale scale
		Company policies and guidelines	1–4 Employee morale scale
		Company values (observed in top management and leaders)	1–4 Employee morale scale
		Work flexibility (schedule, etc.)	1–4 Employee morale scale

3.11   Contingent valuation: Making investment decisions on human capital

Nunes describes this method as an economic, nonmarket-based valuation method especially used to infer the individual's preferences for public goods (Nunes 2013). The origin of this method goes back to when Ciriacy-Wantrup (1947) published the concept of the Contingent Valuation method in an article that focuses on the valuation of the economic effects of preventing soil erosion. However, the first design and implementation of Contingent Valuation took place two decades later when Robert Davis explored the survey technique as part of his PhD dissertation (Davis 1963).

The Contingent Valuation technique provides a mechanism to prioritize employee morale improvements and investment decisions on human capital based on the employee's WTP. In a nutshell, employees are asked if they would be willing to give up part of their salaries to observe an improvement in employee morale factors. This approach provides a cost-benefit analysis that assists decision makers in knowing the return on investment. This technique involves presenting hypothetical situations to a representative sample of the relevant population in order to elicit information about how much they would be willing to pay for specific benefits. This approach is used to develop a prioritization tool for organizational decision makers and HR managers to decide where to invest and improve the employee morale. This technique has been used by HR managers and organizational leaders as a prioritization approach to make wiser decisions. Considering that employee morale is mostly characterized by qualitative performance measures, a cost-benefit approach, such as Contingent Valuation can quantify the investment in qualitative performance measures. This technique allows employees to express how much they are willing to sacrifice out of their paychecks to get a series of incentives. In a study published in and carried out by Connelly et al. (2004), where they studied hundreds of employer-sponsored childcare programs and interviewed some 1000 employees, they found that employees (even with no children) were willing to pay, on average, $125–$225 a year out of their paychecks to provide childcare on-site. The researchers estimated savings in wages of $150,000 and $250,000 for just two companies that provided on-site day care, but the benefits do not stop there. Indirect improvements, such as reduced turnover, higher productivity, lower absenteeism, and improved company image, are among the other benefits observed using this technique.

3.12   Case example

Pam Rogers, like most corporate leaders, considers employee morale the least important measure when she makes organizational decisions. She is aware that a worker's compensation case can significantly impact her business, so she invests in safety and ergonomics, but she does not measure or consider important employee morale important. While Pam, like many other company leaders, cares about her employees and their basic needs, she does not have an idea of how employee morale is impacting other areas that she cares deeply, such as *profit.*

She is the chief executive officer of a Fortune 500 company that uses a product structure to manage a company with subsidiaries spread all over the United States. While the HR department across all the manufacturing plants collects basic employee morale data, such as turnover and absenteeism, Pam and her HR managers do not have a good understanding of how employee morale is affecting the overall success. It is extremely helpful for business leaders to know in greater detail the factors that have an impact on the overall employee morale universe. Pam, like most of the HR managers, would like to know the employee morale level and the return on investment if she decides to invest in making improvements to employee morale. Pam decides to measure the employee morale in two of her subsidiaries, Plant A and Plant B.

Plant A has 250 full-time employees and 3 manufacturing shifts. The majority of the employee morale performance measures have never been measured in Plant A and Plant B, with the exception of the turnover and absenteeism rate. The employee morale survey (Appendix D) not only evaluates most of the employee morale variables, but also how much an employee is willing to pay to realize an improvement in a specific factor of the environment. It is important that Pam and her HR managers truly want to hear what the employees have to say. This assessment tool should be easily accessible and anonymous. That means hardcopy surveys should be facilitated for workers in the manufacturing lines, and boxes placed in all convenient locations. The survey collects all the qualitative measures.

In Plant A, 18 surveys* were collected, which provided the data for 19 of the 21 variables identified in the employee morale model. The other two variables are absenteeism rate and turnover rate, which often are tracked by HR departments in manufacturing organizations.

---

* To calculate the number of surveys necessary, the power level needs to be identified. The power level represents the chance to duplicate the findings obtained on the experiment; therefore, a low power represents a low probability of producing significant results. Considering that 95% confidence interval is commonly used to develop new experiments, the power level selected depends on the effect size. The power level selected is 0.80 at α of 0.05, and effect size of 0.15 requires a sample size of 17 (Keppel 1994). That explains why 18 surveys were collected.

3.12.1 Data collection of qualitative measures

Figure 3.5 represents the linear membership function obtained from the employee morale survey in Plant A. A linear membership function was selected to mathematically represent the factor variables obtained from the survey because this phenomenon is best approximated using linear modeling constructs. The next scatter diagram shows the linear membership function shape. In the X-axis, the survey scale (1–4) is captured, which in Plant A varies from 1.8 to 3.5. In the Y-axis, the degree of membership is captured. Zero means that it barely belongs to the function and 1 that it fully belongs. Clearly, employees in Plant A have a low involvement level and a high commitment level. Involvement is the lowest value and commitment is the highest factor variable of the 19 indicators measured through the employee morale survey.

The WTP technique is used as part of the survey to generate a prioritization tool and assist Pam and her HR managers to make wiser decisions when it comes to making improvements in human capital. Figure 3.6 shows the amount of money employees in Plant A are willing to invest to realize an improvement in the workplace. The next bar chart combined with the

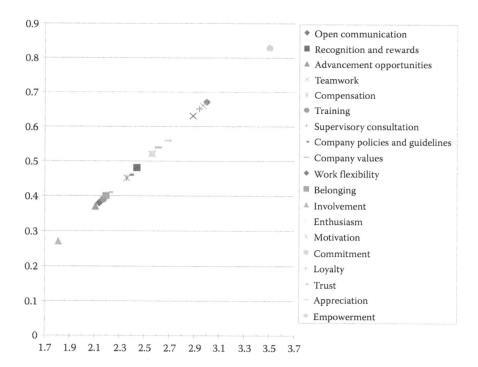

Figure 3.5 Employee moral membership function for manufacturing Plant A.

previous figure provides excellent information that assists Pam and the HR manager in Plant A in knowing the employee morale variables that are holding the business to help accomplish its fullest potential in human capital, and the areas to invest in and get the greatest ROI. While involvement is the lowest variable, it is not a factor that employees are willing to invest heavily in to observe an improvement. However, open communication and advancement opportunities have low levels and employees in Plant A are highly willing to invest to observe an improvement. While many employees often complain about low compensation and are willing to invest to get a salary increase, studies show that compensation is never the most important factor of employee morale. Employees do not change jobs just because another company is offering them more money. It is always something else or a combination of factors that trigger the change.

Figure 3.7 shows a scatter graph with a clear shape that represents a linear membership function for employee morale in Plant B. The lowest

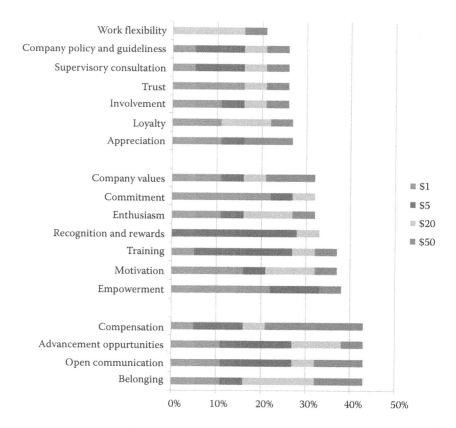

Figure 3.6 WTP for Plant A.

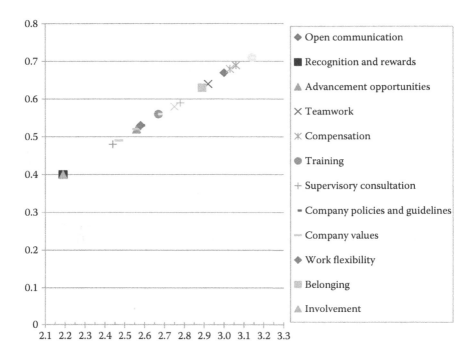

Figure 3.7 Employee morale membership function for manufacturing industry in Plant B.

level of employee morale level is 2.2 and the highest is 3.2. In Plant B, involvement and recognition/rewards are the lowest values while commitment and empowerment are the highest values.

Figure 3.8 shows the bar chart that summarizes the WTP of employees in Plant B to observe an improvement in employee morale. Advancement opportunities and belonging are the areas where employees are more interested in investing. It is interesting to observe that while employees in this site claim to have a high empowerment level, they are also willing to invest in it to be even more empowered.

3.12.2   Data collection of quantitative measures

The U.S. Bureau of Labor Statistics (2008) provides historical data on national averages of absences from work of employed full-time wage and salary workers by occupation and industry, which are used to develop the absenteeism membership function. The idea is to fit the absenteeism rate of Plant A and Plant B in the membership function to know how Pam's subsidiaries are doing with respect to their sector. This membership

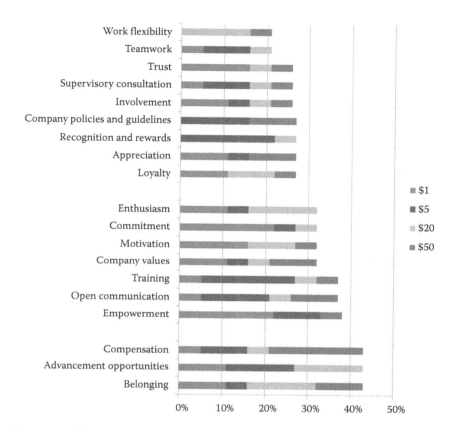

Figure 3.8 WTP for Plant B.

function illustrated in Figure 3.9 represents the absenteeism rate for the manufacturing industry of durable goods. The lower and upper boundaries of the absenteeism membership function are 2.4% and 1.9% absenteeism, respectively. The graph shows that when the absenteeism rate is 2.4%, the degree of membership is 0 so it barely belongs to the function; however, a 1.9% represents an absenteeism rate that fully belongs to the membership function (1 degree of membership). In other words, the lower the percentage of absenteeism, the better.

Pam was surprised to find out that historical data for the past 5 years in Plant A and B show a much higher percentage of absenteeism rate with a minimum of 4.8% and a maximum of 7%. The situation in Plant B was even worse with a minimum of 6.3% and a maximum of 7.9%. When the percentages are fit into the membership function, they all have 0 degree of membership.

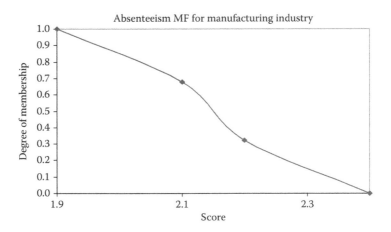

Figure 3.9 Absenteeism membership function.

The U.S. Bureau of Labor Statistics (2007) also publishes the percentages, and annual and monthly figures, of the total separations by industry. The lower and upper boundaries of the turnover membership function are 3.1% and 2.5% turnover, respectively. Figure 3.10 shows that when the turnover rate is 3.1%, the degree of membership is 0 so it barely belongs to the function; however, a 2.5% represents a turnover rate that fully belongs to the membership function (1 degree of membership). Once again, the lower the percentage of turnover rate, the better. This graph is based on national averages in the manufacturing industry and durable goods, which helps Pam and her HR managers to know where they stand. When the turnover rate in Plant A and Plant B for the past 5 years is fitted into the membership function, Pam and her HR managers are surprised to find

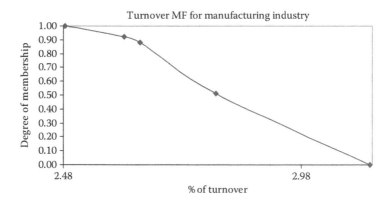

Figure 3.10 Turnover membership function.

out that they are doing poorly. In Plant A, the lowest annual turnover rate is 8.1% and the highest 23%. The situation in Plant B is better, but nevertheless the minimum is 7.4% and the highest 11.2%. These percentages represent a 0 degree of membership. Pam and her HR managers need to work harder to retain their best human capital.

3.12.3 Employee morale index results

Table 3.2 shows the total value of all the employee morale variables (qualitative and quantitative measures) in Plant A and Plant B. These values are obtained by multiplying the degree of membership or Y-axis values by the weights obtained in Figure 3.4. Unfortunately, Pam and her HR managers never measured before the qualitative performance measures so they only have complete data for 1 year. Once they start collecting the data annually, they will be able to predict the future of employee morale in their sites and the impact on the overall company success. After all the weights and degree of membership have been multiplied per variable, all the values are added as the employee morale model states.

Table 3.2 Employee morale total values of Plant A and Plant B

Location	Plant A	Plant B
Absenteeism	0	0
Turnover	0	0
Open communication	0.03	0.05
Recognition and rewards	0.02	0.02
Advancement opportunities	0.02	0.02
Teamwork	0.03	0.03
Compensation	0.03	0.05
Training	0.01	0.02
Supervisory consultation	0.02	0.02
Company policies and guidelines	0.01	0.01
C. values	0.02	0.02
Work flexibility	0.02	0.02
Belonging	0.01	0.02
Involvement	0.01	0.02
Enthusiasm	0.02	0.02
Motivation	0.02	0.02
Commitment	0.04	0.04
Loyalty	0.04	0.04
Trust	0.04	0.06
Appreciation	0.03	0.02
Empowerment	0.05	0.07
Total value of the Ferreras model	*0.47*	*0.57*

3.12.4 *Employee morale index model validation*

The Great Place to Work is the most commonly used approach nowadays to measure employee morale. In fact, business leaders aim every year to be selected. The 2017 list marks Fortune's 20th year of partnering with Great Place to Work to produce the Best Companies to Work For. Therefore, this is selected as the gold standard to validate the Ferreras model. Table 3.3 summarizes the key characteristics of this approach and a checklist was developed to validate the employee morale model (Levering 1988). The checklist was developed based on the following four categories: employment,

Table 3.3 The gold standard checklist

Gold standard checklist			
Basic terms of employment	The job	Workplace rules	Stake in success
1. Fair pay and benefits: (a) compare well with similar employers and (b) square with company's ability to pay	4. Maximizes individual responsibility for how job is done	7. Reduces social and economic distinctions between management and other employees	13. Shares rewards from productivity improvements
2. Commitment to job security	5. Flexibility about working hours	8. Right to due process	14. Shares profits
3. Commitment to safe and attractive working environment	6. Opportunities for growth: a. promotes from within b. provides training c. recognizes mistakes as part of learning	9. Right to information	15. Shares ownership
		10. Right to free speech	16. Shares recognition
		11. Right to confront those in authority	
		12. Right not to be part of the family	

Table 3.4 Gold standard values for Plant A and B

Employee morale assessment		
Question	Plant A	Plant B
1	0.25	0.5
2	0.75	0.75
3	1	0.75
4	0.5	0.75
5	0.75	0.5
6	0.5	0.75
7	0.5	0.75
8	0.5	0.75
9	0.25	0.75
10	0.25	0.75
11	0.25	0.75
12	0.25	0.5
13	0.5	0.25
14	0.5	0.5
15	0.5	0.5
16	0.25	0.25
Total average	*0.46875*	*0.609375*

job, workplace rules, and the stake in success. The complete checklist is included in Appendix E.

The gold standard checklist was used to evaluate the employee morale in Plant A and Plant B, and the results are given in Table 3.4. The employee morale assessment tool provides a unique opportunity to validate the Ferreras model with a very well-known index, the Best Companies to Work For published by Fortune.

Table 3.5 presents the comparison between the Ferreras model and the gold standard, which shows that the Ferreras model has been validated. The scale used to convert all the values is the following: low (0–0.33), medium (0.34–0.66), and high (0.67–1).

The following equation illustrates the accuracy calculation needed for the employee morale index model.

$$\text{Accuracy} = \text{TP} + \text{TN}/(\text{TP} + \text{FP} + \text{FN} + \text{TN}) \tag{3.4}$$

where:
   FP = false-positive
   TN = true-negative
   FN = false-negative
   TP = true-positive

Table 3.5 The Ferreras model versus the gold standard in Plant A and Plant B

Location	Year	Ferreras model	Gold standard
Plant A	2012	Medium	Medium
Plant A	2013	Medium	Medium
Plant A	2014	Medium	Medium
Plant A	2015	Medium	Medium
Plant B	2012	Medium	Medium
Plant B	2013	Medium	Medium
Plant B	2014	Medium	Medium
Plant B	2015	Medium	Medium

Table 3.6 Accuracy values of the Ferreras model

		Gold standard		
Employee morale model		True	False	
	Positive	TP = 8	FP = 0	8/8 = 100%
	Negative	FN = 0	TN = 0	0/0
				Accuracy 8/8 = 100%

The Ferreras model has an accuracy of 100%, which is given in Table 3.6.

3.13   Summary

In conclusion, the Ferreras theory and employee morale index model presented in this chapter are novel approaches that can be used to not only measure and predict the employee morale of any organization, but also to identify the areas to improve and obtain the greatest return on investment. In Chapter 7, the employee morale model is integrated into the company success model.

Janet Flewelling, an expert assisting corporate leaders with HR solutions, states that many business owners believe maintaining morale among employees means they need to offer giveaways, bonuses, and even salary increases. These are temporary solutions, and do not sustain morale. In fact, no salary figure can compensate for low morale. In the twenty-first century, workforce challenges are increasing since more corporations support teleworking and the interactions among employees become more virtual and less in person. Since employees spend on average one-third of their life at work, fostering a work environment that accommodates employee needs is critical. In most cases, employees are eager to contribute to a highly performing and successful firm (Flewelling 2014).

References

Arash. 2014. *The Evolution of HR and the Role of Analytics.* 7Geese. July 17, https://7geese.com/the-evolution-of-hr-and-the-role-of-analytics/

Barney, J. B. 1986. Organizational culture: Can it be a source of sustained competitive advantage? *Academy of Management Review,* 11, 656–665.

Blankenship, M. 2014. *The High Cost of Low Morale by Nicole Fink.* Wesleyan College. July 3, http://go.roberts.edu/bid/183778/The-High-Cost-of-Low-Morale-by-Nicole-Fink

Buchanan, L. 2011. *How SAS Continues to Grow.* INC Magazine. September, http://www.inc.com/magazine/201109/inc-500-james-goodnight-sas.html

Business Dictionary. 2015. *Turnover.* Copyright WebFinance, Inc http://www.businessdictionary.com/definition/turnover.html#ixzz3Zs900fXK

Butters, K. 2013. *Morale Company Culture.* Elcom Blog. September 1, http://www.elcomcms.com/en-au/Resources/Elcom-Blog/Posts/the-importance-of-culture-and-morale-in-the-workplace

Carpenter, M., T. Bauer, and B. Erdogan. 2009. *Principles of Management,* Version 1.0. Flat World Education, Inc.

Ciriacy-Wantrup, S. V. 1947. Capital returns from soil conservation practices. *Journal of Farms Economics,* 29, 1180–1190.

Colburn, K. 2015. *How the Morale of Employees Impacts the Level of Customer Satisfaction.* AccuPOS Blog. http://www.blog.accupos.com/how-the-morale-of-employees-impacts-the-level-of-customer-satisfaction/

Connelly, R., D. S. DeGraff, and R. A. Willis. 2004. *Kids at Work: The Value of Employer-Sponsored On-Site Child Care Centers.* Kalamazoo, MI: W. E. Upjohn Institute.

Corporate Leadership Council. 2013. *Linking Employee Satisfaction with Productivity, Performance, and Customer Satisfaction.* July, http://www.keepem.com/doc_files/clc_articl_on_productivity.pdf

Crowley, M. C. 2013. *How SAS Became the World's Best Place to Work.* Fast Company. January 22, http://www.fastcompany.com/3004953/how-sas-became-worlds-best-place-work

Davis, R. K. 1963. *The Value of Outdoor Recreation: An Economic Study of the Maine Woods.* PhD dissertation, Harvard University, Cambridge, MA.

Dictionary.com. 2015. *Belonging.* September 1, http://dictionary.reference.com/browse/belongingness Dictionary.com. 2015.

Flewelling, J. 2014. *Investing in Employee Morale is Key to a Company's Success.* Score. May 30, https://www.score.org/blog/2014/janet-flewelling/investing-employee-morale-key-company%E2%80%99s-success

Folger, J. 2015. *The Causes and Costs of Absenteeism.* Investopedia. Accessed November 8, 2015. http://www.investopedia.com/articles/personal-finance/070513/causes-and-costs-absenteeism.asp#ixzz3qwvjWjlO

Gallup Consulting®, Harter, J. K., L. Schmidt, E. A. Killham, and J. W. Asplund. 2012. *Q12 Meta-Analysis.* Washington, DC: Gallup Inc.

Grimsley, S. 2015. *What Is Human Capital?—Importance to an Organization.* Accessed September 1, 2015. Study.com. http://study.com/academy/lesson/what-is-human-capital-importance-to-an-organization.html

Hassell, D. 2014. *Open Communication: Vital to Business Success.* San Francisco, CA: American Management Association, September 24.

HR Focus. 2007. Why culture can mean life or death for your organization. *HR Focus* 84, 9.

IThound. 2007. *Human Capital—An Organisation's Most Valuable Intangible Asset.* Ceridian, UK. January, http://www.ithound.com/abstract/human-capital-organisation-valuable-intangible-asset-526

Javitch, D. G. 2005. *Improving Employee Morale.* Entrepreneur. January 2, http://www.entrepreneur.com/article/82710

Keppel, G. 1994. *Design and Analysis: A Researcher's Handbook*, 3rd edition. Englewood Cliffs, NJ: Prentice Hall, pp. 70–82.

Levering, R. 1988. *A Great Place to Work*, 1st edition. New York: Random House.

Manker, A. D. 2015. *Open Communication in the Workplace: Definition, Skills & Benefits.* September 30, Study.com http://study.com/academy/lesson/open-communication-in-the-workplace-definition-skills-benefits.html

Maslow, A. H. 1943. A theory of human motivation. *Psychological Review*, 50, 370–396.

Morgan, L. 2015. *Causes of Low Employee Morale.* Houston Chronicle. Hearst Newspapers. Accessed October 26, 2015.

Nunes, P. A. 2013. *Contingent Valuation Method.* Accessed on November 8, 2015. http://www.coastalwiki.org/wiki/Contingent_Valuation_Method.

Seidman, D. 2012. *(Almost) Everything We Think about Employee Engagement Is Wrong.* Forbes. September 20, http://www.forbes.com/sites/dovseidman/2012/09/20/everything-we-think-about-employee-engagement-is-wrong/

TRC. 2012. *Criteria for Selecting Fortune's Best Companies to Work for.* Workforce Watercooler. January 20, http://workforcewatercooler.com/2012/01/20/criteria-for-selecting-fortunes-best-companies-to-work-for/

U.S. Bureau of Labor Statistics. 2007. Total separations. Accessed June 3, 2007, http://www.bls.gov.

U.S. Bureau of Labor Statistics. 2008. Absences from work. Accessed January 30, 2008. http://www.bls.gov.

Van Rooy, D. L. and K. Oehler. 2013. *The Evolution of Employee Opinion Surveys: The Voice of Employees as A Strategic Business Management Tool.* SHRM-SIOP White Paper Series. Copyright 2013 Society for Human Resource Management. https://www.shrm.org/Research/Articles/Documents/SIOP%20%20Employee%20Engagement%20final.pdf

Williams, D. K. 2013. *The Most Valuable Business Commodity: Trust.* Forbes, Entrepreneurs. June 20, http://www.forbes.com/sites/davidkwilliams/2013/06/20/the-most-valuable-business-commodity-trust/

World Bank. 2011. PovertyNet. http://web.worldbank.org/WBSITE/EXTERNAL/TOPICS/EXTPOVERTY/EXTEMPOWERMENT/0,,contentMDK:20245753~pagePK:210058~piPK:210062~theSitePK:486411,00.html

World Economic Forum and PwC. 2015. *The Evolution of Trust in Business from Delivery to Values.* January, http://www3.weforum.org/docs/WEF_Evolution TrustBusinessDeliveryValues_report_2015.pdf

chapter four

Modeling quality using quantitative and qualitative performance measures

Organizational leaders do not usually consider quality the most important factor of business success or the least important one, but vital. It is a major characteristic of business competitiveness and that is why it is considered critically important for any successful business. While most organizational leaders consider quality a main component of company success, they would rarely consider it their highest priority. Quality often becomes the No. 1 priority for a company leader when it goes one on one with safety. That is the case of pharmaceutical companies, food producers, and the aircraft industry, among others. The nature of the goods manufactured is what triggers the relevance or importance of quality. Quality often becomes a top priority for leaders in enterprises that make products that might jeopardize customers' lives. While some products do not threaten the customer's life, others do and a defect (Type II error in quality) might be the end of the company. The higher the product's liability, the greater the importance quality plays in the mindset of a business leader.

In 1931, Walter Shewhart defined quality as the goodness of a product (Evans and Lindsay 2002). However, quality experts from different sectors have never agreed on a universal definition of quality. The lack of a consistent definition of quality only makes it harder to be measured. Also, quality often entails criteria and standards that are not consistent among users or customers. There are many criteria in quality: customer or user-based, product-based, value-based, and manufacturing-based, among others. What is especially relevant for American makers are the manufacturing-based criteria, which typically represent *conformance to specifications* and the customer-based criteria, where quality is determined by *what the customer wants*. In the quality arena, *specifications* are targets or tolerances determined by product designers to meet the customer's expectations.

It was not until 1978 that the American National Standards Institute (ANSI) and the American Society for Quality (ASQ) came with the official definition of *Quality—the totality of features and characteristics of a product that bears on its ability to satisfy given needs* (ANSI/ASQ 1978).

Cecilia Kimberlin, the 2015 chair of ASQ—the largest professional society in the world of quality experts and practitioners—states that quality is essential to brand development and loyalty. There are plenty of innovative products that lack quality and consequently, they have not successfully sustained. Cecilia claims that in an age of instantaneous public media, quality issues have sent stock prices spiraling downward. Organizations have lost credibility with stakeholders and brand loyalty when they have failed to deliver quality (American Society for Quality 2015).

Quality in the twenty-first century is getting even more challenging due to the advantages in technology and material sciences. Advance manufacturing, smart manufacturing, additive manufacturing, and 3D (three-dimensional) printing are revolutionizing many areas of production businesses, and quality is one of them. The integration of new technological advances and materials is leading to changes in manufacturing processes and, consequently, new challenges in quality control and standards. In fact, there are no quality standards in additive manufacturing where processes have not been yet standardized. If that was not enough, customers are getting more selective and want customized products.

According to the White House Office of Consumer Affairs as reported by *Return on Behavior* magazine (Aksu 2013):

- Overall, 78% of consumers have ended a transaction due to bad service
- Loyal customers are worth up to 10 times as much as their first purchase
- The probability of selling to a new customer is 5%–20% while selling to an existing customer is 60%–70%
- It takes 12 positive experiences to make up for a single bad experience
- Negative interactions with a business are spread to twice as many people as positive ones
- It costs over 6 times more to get new customers than keeping the current ones
- For every customer who complains, 26 others do not speak up

This chapter reviews the relevance of quality and the important role that it plays in the success of manufacturing businesses. This chapter also presents a new quality model that analyzes and combines the qualitative and quantitative performance measures essential for quality success. Specifically, the holistic model introduced in this chapter can assist organizational managers and quality leaders in measuring, evaluating, and predicting quality using a customer driven and financial perspective.

4.1   The evolution of quality

The first sign of quality was found in Egypt in 1450 BC through the evidence of measurement and inspection in wall paintings. The Egyptian pyramids are a living proof of quality. The Egyptians developed methods and procedures that were consistent, precise, and successful: key characteristics for quality.

During the Middle Ages in Europe, individuals who crafted the product wore two hats, the maker and the inspector or auditor. They had so much ownership that they ensured that the product had the highest quality by the maker. Quality was informal, but the situation changed with the industrial revolution.

During the eighteenth century, a French gunsmith, Honoré Le Blanc, developed the concept of interchangeable parts and realized that variation exists in standardized processes. It was then, during the industrial revolution, that *quality assurance* became an integral part of the production process.

In the early 1900s, quality assurance relied on inspectors who represented quality control during the first half of the century. Henry Ford, Sr., one of the leaders of the industrial revolution, developed many of the fundamentals of *total quality practices* in the early 1900s. Henry Ford and Samuel Crowther (1926) published *My Life and Work*, which was defined in Japan as the Bible for quality. Ironically enough, Ford executives realized it in 1982 when they visited Japan to learn from their quality success. When they returned to the United States, they had to go to a bookstore of used books to find a copy. The Bell System was the company to develop the first inspection department in the United States where the first signs of industrial quality assurance was observed. The department gathered the best quality experts of the era that ended developing *quality assurance* and many techniques that still used today. Quality gurus, such as Walter Shewhart and W. Edwards Deming, were part of this group. Shewhart is considered the father of control charts and many other statistical techniques developed under the *statistical quality control* movement. Deming is also considered one of the most influential quality experts in the history along with Juran.

During the 1940s and 1950s, quality was in the hands of specialized experts and organizational leaders. During World War II, statistical sampling and standards on suppliers were implemented by the U.S. military, and statistical quality control was adopted in the manufacturing industry. In the 1960s, Japanese products were internationally known for bad quality, but in 20 years they surpassed western manufacturers under the leadership of the most well-known quality gurus in the history, Edward Deming and Joseph Juran, two American statisticians who were ignored in their home country, but very much listed in Japan where they developed the *continuous improvement* movement or Kaizen (in Japanese). Juran and Deming were not prophets in their own land, but they became quality gurus in Japan. Under their guidance, Japanese products penetrated the global market in a few years. In 30 years, Deming transformed the quality of Japanese products, and was then asked to come back home and improve the quality of American products.

By the 1980s, extensive product recalls and consumer reports made the U.S. government set safety regulations, which elevated the visibility and importance of quality. Customers started to look at products more carefully, making sure that they were getting the best quality for their money. It was then that organizational leaders got the message. Measuring, evaluating, and including quality in organizational decisions was no longer an option but a requirement.

As an effort to improve the level of productivity and quality across American organizations, President Reagan approved the Malcolm Baldrige National Quality Award in 1982. In 1987, the award was established by a Congressional Act. This national award recognizes performance excellence within the quality field in six sectors: manufacturing, service, small business, healthcare, education, and nonprofit. In fact, the Malcolm Baldrige criteria have become widely used as a benchmarking analysis to continuously improve organizations and it is the highest recognition an American organization can receive for performance excellence in quality. The 2015–2016 award criteria were designed to recognize performance excellence within seven categories: leadership, strategy, customers, measurement and analysis, knowledge management, workforce, and results. The framework uses a systems approach to improve organizational performance. In 1990, this award criteria set quality as a principal driver of business success and has been used to enhance a company's competitiveness since then. Finally, managers realized the importance of quality at the leadership and strategic level and elevated it to the point of considering quality management as important as the management of quality. The first organization recognized with a Malcolm Baldrige award was in 1988 (Newman 2014).

Organizational leaders started then to integrate quality principles into their management systems, which led to the development of total quality management (TQM). In the effort of implementing it, many businesses failed. In fact, TQM represents the basics of high-performance management systems.

The European Foundation for Quality Management (EFQM) developed a model to achieve organizational excellence as well, which was introduced as the European Quality Award criteria in 1992. The European model for business excellence has become the most important quality excellence framework in Europe, just like the Malcolm Baldrige National Quality award in the United States. The EFQM model of excellence has been widely

Table 4.1 Six sigma summary table

Sigma level	Defects per million	Yield
6	3.4	99.99966%
5	230	99.977%
4	6210	99.38%
3	66,800	93.32%
2	308,000	69.15%
1	690,000	30.85%

used by many European organizations as a self-assessment tool to enhance organizational performance, and it presents a logical interpretation by grouping a few areas as organizational "enablers" (aim to pursue mission goals and objectives) and others as "results" (real objective of the assessment). The EFQM developed a model that consists of nine criteria points: five are grouped as "enablers" (leadership, people, policy and strategy, partnerships and resources, and process) and the other four are grouped as "results" (people results, customer results, society results, and key performance results). This model provides a great criterion to achieve quality excellence through a feedback mechanism between enablers and results, but fails to provide an approach to achieve company success based on organizational performance measures (Neely et al. 2005; Truccolo et al. 2005).

The last movement in the quality field that remains very present nowadays is Six Sigma, a continuous improvement methodology developed by Motorola leaders Bill Smith and Bob Galvin in 1986. Six Sigma focuses on continuous improvement by obtaining a quality level of at most 3.4 defects per million (DPM) opportunities. Table 4.1 shows the sigma levels, and their respective DPM and yield. Once the performance of the process is measured, the organization wants to continuously improve the sigma level aiming to achieve the 6-sigma level. Even if 6-sigma is never achieved, the improvements that help a company to achieve 4-sigma or 5-sigma will lead the business to reduce costs and increase customer satisfaction (Six Sigma 2016).

4.2 Understanding quality in manufacturing organizations

Quality in manufacturing organizations used to rely on technical tasks such as inspection, process control, calibration, metrology, etc. However, organizations have become customer-driven. This shift has generated changes in manufacturing practices, and that is the case with product development and green manufacturing, among others. While there are many ways of managing quality, an overall quality system must be adopted and implemented. In many cases, the organizational structure determines the quality system to be adopted.

Quality in a manufacturing business represents, more than anything else, the quality of the good or product. An excellent customer service cannot make up for a bad product in a manufacturing business.

Before measuring quality or making any change in that department, it is important to understand the quality system and practices used by the organization. Quality must be considered a core function of the business and must be exemplified by its leaders and managers. Leaders and managers must exemplify and aim for top quality products, processes, and practices or they cannot expect their workers to do it without them leading by example. Quality must be embedded in the business culture. The quality management system in place should be appropriate for the organizational structure selected.

How many times have you seen a manager or a worker under pressure just letting a defect go when it was clearly identified? Actually, it happens frequently. Often, leaders say they deeply care about quality and aim for quality excellence, but their actions send a different message to their subordinates. Quality is reflected by employees' actions and that is why workers are considered "internal customers" and "process owners" in the quality field. Business leaders want their employees feel ownership for their work, independently the position or role they play in the enterprise. However, leading by example is more relevant for those in leadership and management positions. Frequently, business leaders and managers pursue quick fixes without getting to the root cause of the problem. This type of organizations always struggles to attain quality excellence since they are more reactive than proactive. These leaders do not realize that they are just treating the symptoms, not the illness.

When measuring quality, a series of questions should be asked. What type of quality system or philosophy is used? Is it appropriate considering the type of organizational structure? Which performance measures and metrics are collected? What type of inspection and quality standards are in place? What type of data collection tools, methods, and techniques are used? How is continuous improvement ensured? Is the data collected, analyzed, and used to make better decisions? Is the organization rewarding quality workers? Do workers take ownership in producing high-quality products?

4.3 Systems thinking

Quality is a complex system. Processes, materials, standards, employees, and customers, among others, are interrelated to generate goods. Managers and leaders in quality departments need to look at the enterprise as a total quality system, and take into account internal and external factors that affect manufacturing processes. There are many internal and external factors that affect quality, such as suppliers, employees, customers, and competitors, among others. However, organizations must be proactive and minimize as much as possible changes in external factors. For example, suppliers' certification and training truly help manufacturing businesses minimize quality issues. The same applies to outsourced companies that must meet the customer standards. Flexibility is key to adapting quickly and effectively to unforeseen changes.

While variation is inherent in any process, processes must be stable. Otherwise, quality cannot be controlled. A stable process exhibits only common causes of variation. A stable process is predictable or consistent, and the process is considered statistically controlled. Special causes of variation are not part of the process. They can be identified and eliminated. Shewhart is the father of control charts, and these statistical quality control tools were designed to assist in improving processes. When a process has a special cause of variation, the process is out of control. A process out of control is unpredictable (Reference for Business 2015).

While the ultimate goal of any business leader is to please the customers, products before they reach the hands of the users pass through many processes, departments, and hands (internal and external) that add value to the good. The ultimate decider of value added is the customer, who often decides based on the relationship of customer satisfaction and price. Unfortunately, the combination of best practices done separately does not necessarily lead to a good quality system. Business leaders and quality managers must focus on the interactions with other systems in order to obtain quality excellence. It is only by treating quality as a complex system or a subsystem of company success that can be adequately managed that the company products achieve excellence. This approach evaluates quality as an organizational performance measure that fits into a bigger picture, which is company success. Quality must be treated as an essential and vital system for long-term organizational success. A systems approach ensures a holistic and multifaceted analysis of quality.

4.4   Quality for business leaders

While all business leaders look at some type of quality measures, it is strange to find a CEO who considers quality the first priority when making organizational decisions. Juran, one of the greatest quality gurus in history, noticed that when quality problems are presented to leaders in the form of U.S. dollars, top management gets it. The challenge of having a holistic perspective of quality is that a series of quantitative and qualitative measures must be taken into account. Business leaders in the twenty-first century are recognizing that in order to be successful, quality management systems must be customer oriented.

Company leaders often try to convert everything they can into dollars, and that includes quality. While different financial approaches exist in the quality field, the most well-known technique is the "Cost of Quality" (CoQ). This approach is often used by quality managers and company leaders to prioritize the improvement and effectiveness of total quality efforts. The concept of CoQ emerged in the 1950s to characterize quality beyond traditional financial measures, such as the cost of inspection and auditing. The highlight of this approach is that it uses the same language corporate leaders and managers' use. The CoQ is not the price of creating a quality product or service. Instead, it is the cost of not creating a quality product/service or the cost of poor quality. The CoQ is the total cost incurred by

1. Investing in the prevention of nonconformance to requirements
2. Appraising a product or service for conformance to requirements
3. Failing to meet requirements (Campanella 1999)

To implement this approach, the quality activities that generate a cost must be identified. Data must be collected, analyzed, and areas for continuous improvement identified.

Prevention costs arise from efforts to keep defects from occurring within products, processes, or services, which include quality planning, statistical process control, investment in quality-related information systems, quality training and workforce development, product-design verification, and systems development and management.

Appraisal costs are generated from detecting defects via inspection, test, audit test, and inspection of purchased materials. For example, some appraisal cost factors are acceptance testing, inspection, testing, checking labor, setup for test or inspection, test and inspection equipment, quality audits, and field testing.

Internal failure costs are the costs of failure or nonconformance, which arise from defects caught internally and dealt with by discarding or repairing the defective items before they leave the manufacturing plant; for example, scrap, rework, and material procurement costs.

External failure costs come from defective products or services that actually reach customers, such as complaints in warranty, complaints out of warranty, product service, product liability, product recall, and loss of reputation (Evans and Lindsay 2002).

Experts claim that most of the quality costs in manufacturing businesses are generated by internal and external failure costs.

By the end of the 1980s, corporate leaders started realizing that quality could not be conceived without customers. Organizational leaders started integrating customer-driven approaches in their business strategies and management systems. The definition of quality then became very pragmatic—meeting or exceeding customer expectations. Indicators such as customer satisfaction and customer loyalty became a must. This chapter proposes a quality model where financial indicators and customer measures are combined to evaluate and predict quality in manufacturing organizations.

4.5 Limitations of quality models, methods, and techniques

While experts have produced a lot of models, awards, and standards to measure and reward quality excellence in manufacturing organizations, there is no quality index that quantifies quality holistically using six indicators. Most manufacturing organizations have extensive performance measures based on financial accounting systems and do not enable continuous improvement (Bititci 1993). McNair and Masconi (1987), Drucker (1990), and Russell (1992) identified the need for alignment of financial and nonfinancial measures in an organizational framework.

On the basis of research carried out by Bititci and Swenson (1993), Blenkinsop and Burns (1991), and Gelders et al. (1993), there is evidence that even companies that are quality oriented do not have a truly integrated performance measures system. Error is inherited in any process. While a company might not have major quality issues, leaders cannot stop measuring and continuously improving quality just because it is not part of the strategic plan. Strategic plans tend to address current or future priorities, and quality is not always included.

The Malcolm Baldrige National Quality award in the United States has a broad emphasis on customer satisfaction through implementation of total quality management. The Malcolm Baldrige National Quality award recognizes business excellence based on seven categories: leadership, strategic planning, customer–market focus, information analysis, human resources focus, and process (Neely et al. 2005). Also, the EFQM model provides a great approach to achieve quality excellence through a feedback mechanism between enablers and results. Enablers and their respective weight are leadership—10%, people—9%, policy and strategy—8%, partnerships and resources—9%, and process—14%. Results and their weights are considered to be people results—9%, customer results—20%, society results—6%, and key performance results—15% (Truccolo et al. 2005). Leadership is the key criterion for the Baldrige award and the EFQM model, and both use a weighted approach (Nakhai and Neves 1994). These models put a lot of importance on leadership and strategic plans rather than on the ability of any business to thrive through success.

All the approaches and techniques discussed have something in common. They are (1) assume the achievement of a strategic plan represents business success, (2) assume all strategic plans are good and all businesses have one, (3) assume quality is always included in any strategic plan or objectives, (4) do not necessarily provide a set of comprehensive metrics, (5) do not necessarily take into account continuous improvement, (6) do not necessarily combine quantitative and qualitative measures to assess quality success, and (7) do not necessarily fit into a more holistic or multifaceted model.

4.6 Analyzing quality in manufacturing organizations using a holistic approach

Since quality is a complex topic for a manufacturing organization, the use of a taxonomy to disengage the complexity of the characterization process is ideal. The purpose of developing a taxonomy is to simplify and assist the characterization process when a complex problem needs to be solved. The taxonomy structure follows a configuration which facilitates the process of breaking a complex problem into subcomponents, leading to a simplistic way to identify the key performance measures affecting quality. This chapter presents a taxonomy to appropriately measure and evaluate quality in manufacturing businesses. Literature review and SMEs facilitated the characterization. Figure 4.1 illustrates the quality taxonomy, with the structure of component, subcomponent, and factor variables. The external factors are mainly dominated by the customer. All companies can aim to achieve 100% customer satisfaction, but attaining it is a different story. The internal factors focus on achieving excellence in quality management and quality control key performance measures, such as appraisal and prevention efforts.

The taxonomy identifies the following key performance measures that are essential to measure quality holistically in manufacturing organizations:

- *Customer loyalty* is measured by the percentage of repeat customers based on the annual amount spent.

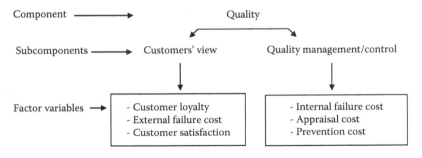

Figure 4.1 Quality categorization structure.

- *Customer satisfaction* is captured by the percentage of satisfied customers.
- *External failure costs*
  - Costs due to customer complaints and returns, which includes rework on returned items, cancelled orders, and freight premiums.
  - Product recall costs and warranty claims, such as the cost of repair, replacement associated administrative costs, etc.
  - Product liability costs often result from legal actions and settlements.
- *Internal failure costs*
  - Scrap and rework costs, including material, labor, and overhead.
  - Costs of corrective action arise from time spent determining the causes of failure and correcting production problems.
  - Downgrading costs, such as including revenue lost when selling a product at a lower price when it does not meet specifications.
  - Process failure costs, including unplanned machine downtime or unplanned equipment repair.
- *Appraisal costs*
  - Test and inspection costs, such as those associated with incoming materials, work-in-process, and finished goods (including equipment costs and salaries).
  - Instrument maintenance costs arise from calibration and repair of measuring instruments.
  - Process measurement and control costs include the time spent by workers to gather and analyze quality measurements.
- *Prevention costs*
  - Quality planning costs include salaries of individuals associated with quality planning and problem-solving teams, the development of new procedures, new equipment design, and reliability studies.
  - Process control costs entail costs spent on analyzing production processes and implementing process control plans.
  - Information systems costs, such as expenses to develop data requirements and measurements.
  - Training and general management costs, including internal and external training programs, clerical staff expenses (secretarial or assistant), and miscellaneous supplies (Harrington 1987; Evans and Lindsay 2002).

4.6.1 Customers' view

Probably the best definition of quality in a customer-driven business is meeting or exceeding customer expectations. When customer' expectations are not met, then there is a dissatisfied customer. It is as simple as that. A product might be innovative and have good quality, but if it does not meet or exceed customer expectations, there is an unhappy customer.

TeleFaction A/S (2009), a Danish company pioneer on customer experience management, identified 23 facts that cannot be ignored about customers' loyalty and satisfaction. Also, James Digby (2010) compiled 50 facts about customer experience that every company leader and quality manager should be aware of. A selection of the key facts is listed below:

- Overall, 96% of unhappy customers do not complain; however, 91% of those will simply leave and never come back.
- Around 90% of unhappy customers will not buy again from a company that disappointed them.
- A dissatisfied customer will tell 9–15 people about their experience.
- Around 13% of dissatisfied customers tell more than 20 people.
- It takes 12 good experiences to make up for a bad one.
- Dissatisfied customers whose complaints are taken care of are more likely to remain loyal, and even become advocates, than those who are "just" customers.
- Overall, 70% of buying experiences are based on how the customer feels they are being treated.
- A good customer experience is shared with eight others.
- A typical company receives around 65% of its business from existing customers.
- An average company loses between 10% and 30% of its customers each year.
- Overall, 7 out of 10 customers switching to a competitor do so because of poor service.
- Satisfying and retaining current customers is 3–10 times cheaper than acquiring new customers.
- A 2% increase in customer retention has the same effect as decreasing costs by 10%.
- A 5% reduction in the customer defection rate can increase profits by 25% to 80%.

These facts make clear the importance of customer satisfaction and customer loyalty. Organizational leaders are realizing that customer-driven businesses are more successful than others, and Bob Wise, president of FreeConferenceCall.com, is one of them. While many companies today are focusing on becoming customer-centric enterprises to achieve sustainable success, very few company leaders use business models that require it. Bob states that entrepreneurs and business leaders can never go wrong by focusing on customers' needs, earning their loyalty, and following their lead into new markets. While it is easy to develop a customer-friendly mission, it is hard to stick to it under revenue pressure from markets, boards, and investors (Wise 2015). Netflix, a company that put Blockbuster out of business, is a great example. Netflix was charging $10/month for a combo plan (DVD-by-mail and online streaming) and in an attempt to increase revenues, the company forced customers in 2011 to choose just one service or pay $16. The 60% price increase was not well received by the customers, even though Netflix offered customers a choice between paying $8 a month for the DVD service alone or $8/month for the streaming service. According to the Young Entrepreneurs Council, that decision ended costing them more than a million customers and 50% of their company value at the time (Young Entrepreneurs Council 2011).

Zara, the retail clothing business, has been able to demonstrate that it is customer-centric. Zara's customers make on average 17 annual store visits, compared to 4 visits for other retailers. As a result, 85% of Zara's inventory sells at full price compared to a retail average of 40%. As a result Zara hardly spends in advertising (only 0.3% of sales) compared to (3–4% of sales) competitors. Zara's customers pass frequently to see what is new, and end up buying because they are afraid they might never find the item they want in their size the next time they pass by the store (Bliss 2011).

All businesses should always aim to deliver the best customer experiences. Leaders of the Ritz Carlton never sacrifice quality, not even during recession years when the market suffers. As a result, they experience an increase in customers when others cut or reduce their quality experience. This is often observed in commercial airlines, where quality has decreased as an approach to make up for the gas price increase. As a consequence, airlines like the United Emirates or Turkish Airlines, which provide more and better products and services, are now considered to have better quality than American carriers. In fact, 71% of business leaders believe that customer experience is the next corporate battleground (Shaw and Ivens 2002).

Business Wire published in 2012 a summary of the annual customer experience impact (CEI) report conducted by Harris Interactive on behalf of RightNow where over 2,291 U.S. adults were surveyed. Apparently, 86% of American adults are willing to pay more for a better customer experience and 89% who stopped doing business with an organization due to a poor customer experience began doing business with a competitor. Actually, 54% of the customers agreed that improving the overall customer experience is the best way companies can engage them to spend more.

The CEI report also shows the important role social media plays for dissatisfied consumers. Apparently, 26% of U.S. adults expressed frustration by posting a negative comment on a social networking site after a poor customer experience and 79% of those who shared complaints about poor customer experience online had their complaints ignored. The good news is that of those surveyed who received a response, 57% had positive reactions to the same company, 46% were pleased, and 22% posted a positive comment about the organization afterward.

Positive engagements create longstanding and loyal relationships. As the CEI report discloses, consumers are willing to pay for it. To maximize this opportunity, organizations today need to implement comprehensive and customer experience programs to meet the constantly evolving needs of the modern consumer. Data once again demonstrate that customers nowadays want personalized products, engaging experiences, and are willing to pay for them if offered. Overall, delivering exceptional customer experiences is essential for any organization that wants to grow and sustain competitive differentiation in today's market.

Talkdesk has identified the top 10 customer-centric companies in 2014 based on customer service lists and articles compiled by several organizations, such as Forbes, USA Today, etc. It is not a surprise that Amazon continues to dominate the list since it develops products based on customer desires rather than their development team's opinion. Also, the online retail giant cultivates a culture of metrics where they routinely engage in testing customers' reactions to new features or designs.

According to Joshua Sloser, VP of digital innovation at Hilton, 42% of the hotel guests expect a response to their post on social media within an hour and the percentage increases to 72% if it is a customer service related issue. Hilton has rolled out policies and procedures to help meet these expectations. Furthermore, UPS uses social media as to anticipate customer needs, to provide better customer support and optimize efficiency. Some company leaders think that by just looking at a few quarterly metrics, such as customer complaints, it is enough. Apple's CEO Tim Cook reads customer emails daily. Listening to customers pays off, and it is key for top performers in any sector (Talkdesk 2015).

4.6.2   Quality management and quality control

The first sign of process control was observed in the Egyptian pyramids when a system for quarrying and dressing stone was designed. It was not until the 1920s that TQM began as a term coined by the Naval Air Systems Command to describe its Japanese-style management approach to quality improvement. It is a methodology for continually improve the quality of all processes, and it draws on a knowledge of the principles and practices. The following timeline reviews the major evolution and advancement of quality control and management in the past three centuries:

1700–1900: Quality is largely determined by the efforts of an individual craftsman. Eli Whitney introduces standardized, interchangeable parts to simplify assembly.

1900–1930: Henry Ford—the assembly line—further refinement of work methods to improve productivity and quality; Ford developed mistake-proof assembly concepts, self-checking, and in-process inspection.

1907–1908: AT&T begins systematic inspection and testing of products and materials.

1924: Walter Shewhart introduces the control chart concept in a Bell Laboratories technical memorandum and in 1931, he published *Economic Control of Quality of Manufactured Products*. He is the father of control charts that up to today are used as the basics of quality control.

1930s: W. Edwards Deming developed methods for statistical analysis and control of quality.

1946: The American Society for Quality Control is formed.

1948: Taguchi begins a study and application of experimental design.

1950: Ishikawa introduces the cause-and-effect diagram. W. Edwards Deming becomes popular in Japan.

1951: V. Feigenbaum publishes the first edition of his book, *Total Quality Control* and the Deming Prize is established. Also, Joseph M. Juran publishes the *Quality Control Handbook*. Juran advanced the field by developing the concepts of controlling quality and managerial breakthrough.

1960s: Philip B. Crosby developed the concept of "zero defects" (ZD) and programs are introduced in certain U.S. industries.

1967: Kaoru Ishikawa's synthesis of the philosophy contributed to Japan's ascendancy as a quality leader.

1970: Philip B. Crosby publishes *Quality is Free*.

1980: Ford Motor Company invites Deming to speak to executives. In the 1980s, TQM becomes a popular philosophy for managing organizational quality systemically.

1987: ISO publishes the first quality systems standard. A Six Sigma initiative begins in Motorola.

1987: The Malcolm Baldrige National Quality Award is established by Congress.

1994: The first American Customer Satisfaction Index (ACSI) is released, measuring consumer satisfaction with the quality of goods and services.

1998: The American Society for Quality Control becomes the American Society for Quality.

2000s: The ISO 9000:2000 standard was released. Supply chain management and supplier quality become even more critical factors in business success (ASQ 2015).

Joseph Juran was the first quality guru to discuss the cost of quality analysis and became a pioneer of quality costing. In 1956, Armand

Feigenbaum identified the following quality cost categories: prevention, appraisal, and failure (internal and external) (Dobrin and Stănciuc 2013; Schiffauerova and Thomson 2015).

As previously discussed in this chapter, CoQ is the expense of non-conformance Philip B. Crosby (1979) popularized the use of CoQ in his book *Quality is Free*. Crosby stated that most companies spend 15%–20% of their sales in quality costs. A company with good quality can have a cost of quality that is less than 2.5% of sales, and is primarily spent in prevention and appraisal costs.

Manufacturing businesses must have a good quality management and control program or plan in place that tackles excellence in the internal and controllable factors of quality. While the external factors are uncontrollable, such as customer behavior or disruptive competitors, the in house quality homework must get done. Manufacturing enterprises must achieve quality success through excellent quality management, quality control, and continuous improvement efforts.

4.7   A holistic quality index model

A new quality index model is presented in Equation 4.1 that combines the concept of CoQ with customers' view. Customer factors are also taken into account in the index model that combines qualitative and quantitative measures to assess quality holistically.

The following mathematical model, Equation 4.1, represents a new quality index model developed to evaluate the quality success of manufacturing organizations. Additive mathematical operands are used to group the quality membership functions obtained per factor variable.

$$Q\,(Plant, Year) = (W_{PC} \times PC) + (W_{AC} \times AC) + (W_{IC} \times IC)$$
$$+ (W_{EC} \times EC) + (W_{CS} \times CS) + (W_{CL} \times CL) \qquad (4.1)$$

where:
W_{PC} = weight of *prevention cost*
PC = *prevention cost* degree of membership
W_{AC} = weight of *appraisal cost*
AC = *appraisal cost* degree of membership
W_{IC} = weight of *internal failure cost*
IC = *internal failure cost* degree of membership
W_{EC} = weight of *external failure cost*
EC = *external failure cost* degree of membership
W_{CS} = weight of *customer satisfaction*
CS = *customer satisfaction* degree of membership

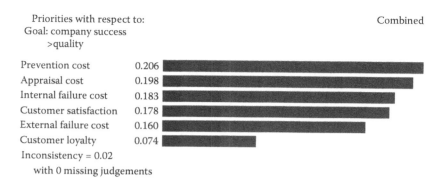

Figure 4.2 Quality index model weights.

W_{CL} = weight of *customer loyalty*
CL = *customer loyalty* degree of membership

4.8 Weights

As discussed in Chapter 2, SMEs from academia and industry were asked to perform a pairwise comparison. Figure 4.2 shows the weights for every factor variable identified in the quality index model. The bar chart shows customer loyalty as the least important variable.

Figure 4.2 comes from Expert Choice, one of the software programs available to calculate the weights using the Analytical Hierarchy Process. The inconsistency ratio identified is 0.02, which shows that subject matter experts were consistent (must be smaller than 0.1).

Table 4.2 provides a summary of the performance measures considered in the quality index model and a clearly defined set of metrics that can be easily evaluated in manufacturing organizations. The following performance measures are based on the concept of CoQ and customers' view.

4.9 Case example

Pam Rogers, like most of the corporate leaders, considers quality an integral part of her business. As chief executive officer of a Fortune 500 solar panel producer, she cares about the quality of her goods since it obviously affects the company's profit and image. She knows that without quality, she will not make it far. Pam's goods are ISO 50001/ISO 9001/ISO 14001 certified, and she does not experience major quality issues. That leads her not to include quality as part of her strategic plan or business priority. Instead, Pam just keeps an eye on two or three performance measures

Table 4.2 Quality performance measures and metrics

Customers' view	Customer loyalty	Percentage of repeated business (customer buying pattern)
	External failure cost	Customer complaints and returns, product recall cost and warranty claims, and product liability cost
	Customer satisfaction	Percentage of customer satisfaction
Quality management/ control	Internal failure cost	Scrap and rework cost, cost of corrective action, downgrading cost, and process failures
	Appraisal cost	Test and inspection cost, instrument maintenance cost, process measurement, and control cost
	Prevention cost	Quality planning cost, process control costs, information systems costs, training and general management cost

in every quality report. Product liability cost, warranty claims, customer complaints, and defects per million (DPM in Six Sigma), among others, are used by many CEOs and corporate leaders in manufacturing industries as quality indicators. Pam knows how broad quality is, and she would like to have a single figure that tells her how good her company and sites are doing in terms of quality. She would like an approach that can not only quickly evaluate quality from a holistic and multifaceted perspective, but also one fits into the bigger picture. Pam would also like to have a tool that can help her identify the areas in quality that are preventing her business from being the market leader.

4.9.1 Data collection and membership function development

The purpose of this step is to identify the quality data available and the data that should be collected. Plant A and Plant B manufacture solar panels. Plant A products are for commercial applications while Plant B products are for residential applications. Therefore, a glossary of terms and a questionnaire for quality managers are great tools to start collecting data and identifying what has been measured, how, and how the data have been analyzed and used. Different sites or manufacturing

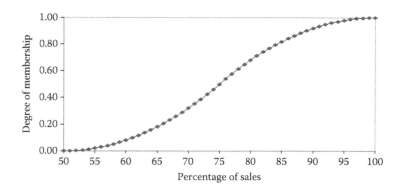

Figure 4.3 Customer loyalty membership function.

plants might be collecting different performance measures. Even though some metrics have never been measured before, such as rework percentage or incoming material inspection, historical data were found for the majority of the performance measures identified as part of the quality index model.

Figure 4.3 shows the customer loyalty membership function developed using a scale identified by SMEs. A sigmoidal membership function was selected to represent customer loyalty. The figure shows that when the loyal customer has a percentage of sales of 50%, the degree of membership is 0, so it barely belongs to the function; however, 100% percentage of sales represents a loyal customer who fully belongs to the membership function because the degree of membership is 1.

Figure 4.4 shows the customer-satisfaction membership function developed using the American Customer Satisfaction Index® published by the ASQ and the CFI Group. The ACSI model was derived from a model originally implemented in 1989 in Sweden called the Swedish Customer Satisfaction Barometer (SCSB). This index is published quarterly and is applied to different industry sectors, such as manufacturing. The national ACSI score measures U.S. overall customer satisfaction and is an aggregation of all sectors and industries measured by the ACSI. The national ACSI score represents the average of all sector scores, weighted by each sector's contribution to the U.S. gross domestic product (GDP). The ACSI conducts more than 70,000 interviews annually (ACSI 2016). A sigmoidal membership function was selected to represent customer loyalty. The figure shows that when the customer is 82% satisfied, the degree of membership is 0, so it barely belongs to the function; however, 100% customer satisfaction fully belongs to the membership function because the degree of membership is 1.

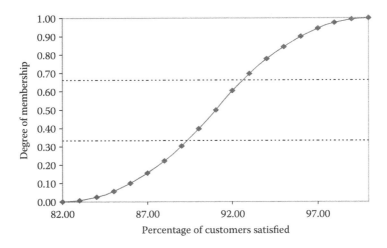

Figure 4.4 Customer satisfaction membership function.

Using SMEs, the scale for the external failure cost membership function was developed. Figure 4.5 shows a sigmoidal membership function, which was used to represent the external failure cost factor variable. The figure shows the x values representing the external failure cost as the percentage of sales, and the y values representing the degree of membership.

Figure 4.5 shows that when the external cost represents 4% of the sales, the degree of membership is 0, so it barely belongs to the function; however, at 0.70% of sales, it fully belongs to the membership function.

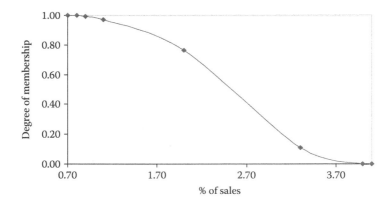

Figure 4.5 External failure cost membership function.

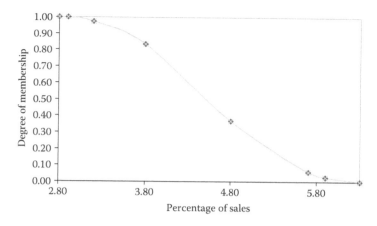

Figure 4.6 Internal failure cost membership function.

Similarly, Figure 4.6 shows the internal failure cost membership function developed using a scale identified by SMEs.

Figure 4.6 shows that when the cost is 6.3% of sales, the degree of membership is 0, so it barely belongs to the function; however, 2.8% of cost as a percentage of sales fully belongs to the membership function because the degree of membership is 1. Figure 4.7 shows the appraisal cost membership function, which is sigmoidal. The function was developed using SMEs' opinions to build the scale.

Figure 4.7 shows that when the appraisal cost is 2.3% of sales, the degree of membership is 0, so it barely belongs to the function; however, a 3.2% of sales fully belongs to the membership function with 1 degree.

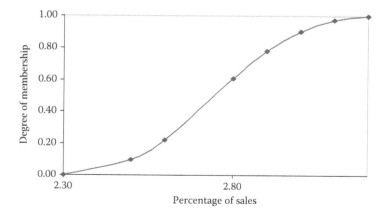

Figure 4.7 Appraisal cost membership function.

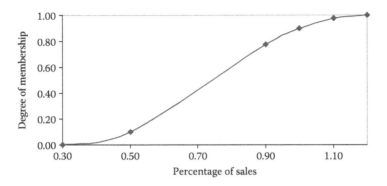

Figure 4.8 Prevention cost membership function.

Building membership functions give us the flexibility to combine all the performance measures into a single index model. Figure 4.8 illustrates the prevention cost membership function and was also developed looking at the percentage of sales, which is represented by a sigmoidal membership function. Figure 4.8 shows that when the prevention cost is 0.3% of sales, the degree of membership is 0, so it barely belongs to the function; however, a cost of 1.2% of sales fully belongs to the membership function since the degree of membership is 1. SMEs identified the scale to build the membership function.

4.9.2   Quality index model results

Table 4.3 summarizes the data obtained from Plant A while Table 4.4 summarizes the data obtained from Plant B. Tools, such as calibration and maintenance reports, continuous improvement projects, customer satisfaction surveys, and warranty claims reports, were used to evaluate Pam's factories. Even though quality managers had never collected data on some performance measures, such as rework percentage or incoming material

Table 4.3 Quality data obtained from Plant A

Subcomp.	Factor variable	2012	2013	2014	2015
Customer satisfaction	Customer loyalty	83.1%	81.05%	79%	76.95%
	External failure cost	$393,041	$428,714	$464,387	$489,491
	Customer satisfaction	91%	90.5%	90%	89.5%
Quality management and control	Internal failure cost	$260,633	$269,027	$262,382	$332,211
	Appraisal cost	$16,000	$7268	$13,777	$10,557
	Prevention cost	$67,688	$46,313	$706	$1638

Table 4.4 Quality data obtained from Plant B

Subcomp.	Factor variables	2012	2013	2014	2015	2016
Customer satisfaction	Customer loyalty	94%	93.73%	93.20%	92.83%	92.63%
	External failure cost	N/A	$336,285	$1,446,108	$1,365,416	$1,752,494
	Customer satisfaction	77.8%	78.4%	77.6%	84.8%	85.2%
Quality management and control	Internal failure cost	$500,000	$578,244	$636,862	$986,904	$1,349,819
	Appraisal cost	$8500	$8500	$8553	$8540	$8709
	Prevention cost	$0	$0	$0	$71,928	$65,232

inspection, historical data were found for the majority of the organizational performance measures identified within the quality model.

As observed in the table, Plant B never collected some of the performance measures identified in the quality index model.

4.9.3 Quality index model validation

Table 4.5 summarizes all the data from membership functions, the total value for each plant per year, and the gold standard. The gold standard selected is CoQ since this approach has been traditionally used as the best way to measure overall quality within organizations.

Table 4.6 provides a summary of the results once the numerical results are converted using the scale (0–0.33 is low, 0.34–0.66 is medium, and

Table 4.5 Quality membership function values versus gold standard for Plant A and Plant B

Location	Year	Prev. cost	Appr. cost	Inter. cost	Exter. cost	Cust. satis.	Cust. loyal.	Total	Gold standard
Plant A	2012	0.0021	0.0020	0.1830	0.1581	0.1665	0.0005	0.5122	0.3452
Plant A	2013	0.0021	0.0020	0.1830	0.1583	0.1651	0.0005	0.5110	0.3453
Plant A	2014	0.0021	0.0020	0.1830	0.1586	0.1638	0.0041	0.5136	0.3457
Plant A	2015	0.0021	0.0020	0.1830	0.1578	0.1623	0.0000	0.5072	0.3449
Plant B	2013	0.0021	0.0020	0.1830	0.1558	0.1116	0.0559	0.5104	0.3429
Plant B	2014	0.0021	0.0020	0.1830	0.1516	0.1065	0.0529	0.4981	0.3387
Plant B	2015	0.0021	0.0020	0.1827	0.1580	0.1451	0.0503	0.5402	0.3447
Plant B	2016	0.0021	0.0020	0.1773	0.1376	0.1468	0.0490	0.5148	0.3190

Table 4.6 Quality model versus gold standard for Plant A and Plant B

Location	Year	Quality model	Gold standard
Plant A	2012	Medium	Medium
Plant A	2013	Medium	Medium
Plant A	2014	Medium	Medium
Plant A	2015	Medium	Medium
Plant B	2013	Medium	Medium
Plant B	2014	Medium	Medium
Plant B	2015	Medium	Medium
Plant B	2016	Medium	Low

Table 4.7 Accuracy of the quality index model

Quality model		Gold standard (CoQ)		
		True	False	
	Positive	TP = 7	FP = 1	$7/(7+1) = 87.5\%$
	Negative	FN = 0	TN = 0	$0/0$
				Accuracy
				$7/8 = 87.5\%$

0.67–1 is high). The quality index model developed shows similar levels as the gold standard.

Table 4.7 shows the validation of the quality index model by calculating its accuracy, which is 87.5%. This validates the quality index model.

4.10   Summary

In this chapter, a new quality index model is presented using the methodology discussed in Chapter 2. The uniqueness of this model is the holistic approach used to characterize quality based on a series of quantitative and qualitative performance measures that fall under two subcomponents: Customers' view and quality management/control. While most companies collect quality measures, such as the number of products returned or warranty claims, many organizations, such as Pam's business, do not collect other measures, such as prevention costs. SMEs and literature review assisted in identifying the scales and weights used to develop the membership functions. This model has been validated and can help quality managers and organizational leaders, making wiser decisions in quality that impact company success. A single figure model that evaluates, predicts, and compares quality excellence across different sites within the same organization or across multiple organizations has been presented in this chapter.

References

ACSI. 2016. Accessed November 26, 2016. http://www.theacsi.org/

Aksu, H. 2013. *Customer Service: The New Proactive Marketing.* The Huff Post, Business. Posted March 26, http://www.huffingtonpost.com/hulya-aksu/customer-service-the-new-_b_2827889.html

American Customer Satisfaction Index. 2016. *ACSI—Manufacturing Durable Goods & Non-Goods.* http://www.theacsi.org/the-american-customer-satisfaction-index

American Society for Quality. 2015. *Future of Quality Report: Quality Throughout.* http://rube.asq.org/2015/05/global-quality/2015-future-of-quality.pdf

ANSI/ASQC. 1978. *Quality Systems Terminology.* Milwaukee, WI: American Society for Quality Control.

ASQ. 2015. *History of Total Quality Management.* Adapted from The Certified Manager of Quality/Organizational Excellence Handbook, pp. 290–291. Accessed November 11, 2015. http://asq.org/learn-about-quality/total-quality-management/overview/tqm-history.html

Bititci, U. S. and H. Swenson. 1993. *Use of Performance Measures at Strategic and Operational Levels.* Unpublished research report, University of Strathclyde, Glasgow, UK.

Bititci, U. S. 1993. Integrated performance measures: The key to business integration and improvement. *9th NCMR,* September.

Blenkinsop, S. and N. D. Burns. 1991. Performance measurement as an integrating factor in manufacturing enterprises. *7th NCMR,* 231–236.

Bliss, J. 2011. *How ZARA Became a Customer Magnet.* 1to1media. May 19, http://www.1to1media.com/weblog/2011/05/guest_blogger_jeanne_bliss_how.html

Campanella, J. 1999. *Principles of Quality Costs,* 3rd Edition. In: *Principles, Implementation, and Use.* Milwaukee, WI: ASQC Quality Press.

Cartin, T. J. 1999. *Principles and Practices of Organizational Performance Excellence.* Milwaukee, WI: ASQ Quality Press.

Crosby, P. B. 1979. *Quality is Free.* New York: McGraw-Hill.

Digby, J. 2010. 50 facts about customer experience. *Return on Behavior Magazine.* Posted October 26, http://returnonbehavior.com/2010/10/50-facts-about-customer-experience-for-2011/

Dobrin, C. and A. M. Stănciuc. 2013. Quality cost system an excellent tool in the overall management business. *Revista Economica,* 65(3), 37–45.

Drucker, P. E. 1990. The emerging theory of manufacturing. *Harvard Business Review,* May/June, 94–102.

Evans, J. R. and W. M. Lindsay. 2002. *The Management and Control of Quality,* 5th edition. Cincinnati, OH: South-Western. Thomson Learning, pp. 115, 462.

Feigenbaum, A. V. 1956. Total quality control. *Harvard Business Review,* 34(6), 93.

Ford, H. and S. Crowther. 1926. *My Life and Work.* New York: Garden City Publishing Co.

Gelders, L., Mannaerts, P., and J. Maes. 1993. Manufacturing strategy and performance indicators. *Proceedings of IEPM'93.* Brussels, Belgium.

Gryna, F. M. 1999. Quality and cost. In: J.M. Juran and A.B. Godfrey (eds), *Juran's Quality Handbook.* New York: McGraw-Hill.

Harrington, H. J. 1987. *Poor-Quality Cost: Implementing, Understanding, and Using the Cost of Poor Quality,* 11th edition. CRC Press. February 26. New York, NY and Milwaukee, Wisconsin.

Juran, J. M. 1951. *Quality Control Handbook,* 1st edition. New York: McGraw-Hill.

McNair, C. J. and W. Mosconi. 1987. Measuring performance in advanced manufacturing environment. *Management Accounting,* July, 28–31.

Nakhai, B. and J. S. Neves. 1994. The Deming, Baldrige, and European Quality Award. *Quality Progress,* 27(4QICID: 12827), April, 33–37.

Neely, A., Gregory, M., and K. Platts. 2005. Performance measurement system design: A literature review and research agenda. *International Journal of Operations & Production Management,* 25(12), 1228–1263.

Newman, M. 2014. *Eligibility Requirements Revised for 2015 Baldrige Award.* NIST Tech Beat. Posted October 6, http://www.nist.gov/baldrige/20141006_eligibiliyrequire_revised.cfm

Reference for Business. 2015. *Statistical Process Control.* Advameg, Inc. www.referenceforbusiness.com/encyclopedia/Sel-Str/Statistical-Process-Control.html

Russell, R. 1992. The role of performance measurement in manufacturing excellence. *BPICS Conference 1992.*

Schiffauerova, A. and V. Thomson. 2015. Cost of quality: A survey of models and best practices. *International Journal of Quality and Reliability Management.* Accessed November 13, 2015. http://www.mcgill.ca/files/mmm/CoQModels-BestPractices.pdf

Shaw, C. and J. Ivens. 2002. *Building Great Customer Experiences.* UK: Palgrave Macmillan.

Six Sigma. 2016. *Lean Manufacturing and Six Sigma Definitions.* Accessed November 25, 2016. http://leansixsigmadefinition.com/glossary/six-sigma/

Talkdesk, Inc. 2015. *Top 10 Customer-Centric Companies of 2014.* Posted on January 13, http://www.talkdesk.com/blog/top-10-customer-centric-companies-of-2014/

TeleFaction A/S. 2009. 23 Facts you can't ignore about customers' loyalty and satisfaction. *Return on Behavior Magazine.* Posted September 26, http://returnonbehavior.com/2009/09/facts-you-cant-ignore/

Truccolo, I., Bianchet, K., Ciolfi, L., Michilin, N., Giacomello, E., Parro, A., Ricci, R., Flego, A., and P. De Paoli. 2005. EFQM and libraries: An organizational challenge for improving the provided services. *EAHIL Workshop, Implementation of Quality Systems and Certification of Biomedical Libraries.*

Wise, B. 2015. *Top Strategies for Creating a Truly Customer-Driven Company.* FreeConference.com. Posted on September 16, http://www.freeconference-call.com/blog/?p=3546

Young Entrepreneurs Council. 2011. *5 Business Lessons from the Netflix Pricing Debacle.* Forbes. Posted December 28, http://www.forbes.com/sites/theyec/2011/12/28/5-business-lessons-from-the-netflix-pricing-debacle/

chapter five

A new model to evaluate and predict ergonomics and safety

Quality has become an important competitive domain that has been seen to have links to ergonomics (Drury 2000). For example, Axelsson (2000) found that jobs with poor ergonomics were 10 times more likely to have quality deficits than jobs with good ergonomics, and Yeow and Sen (2003) found a reduction of $574,000 in rejection costs with less than $1100 in modifications and training, which led to a 5.2% reduction in customer side deficits. These examples illustrate how ergonomics can contribute to strategic quality (Dul 2005).

In "Make More Money by Making Your Employees Happy," Dr. Nelson shares the example of when Paul O'Neil took the reigns of Alcoa AA +0.00% in 1987, the world's leading producer of aluminum. O'Neil announced that his sole priority was to increase worker safety, which was a shock for the board room. He understood that safety was a major concern for his workers. Over the next 13 years, employee productivity soared as accident rates decreased from roughly one per week per plant to some plants going years without an accident. When O'Neil stepped away just over a decade later, Alcoa's annual income had grown 500% (Cooper 2012).

"Managers usually associate ergonomics with occupational health and *Safety* and related legislation, not with business performance. In many companies, these decision makers seem not to be positively motivated to apply ergonomics for reasons of improving health and safety" (Dul and Neumann 2008:1). While decisions made by organizational leaders are not frequently studied from an ergonomics perspective, nevertheless they can have a considerable impact on the working conditions for the entire workforce. The reverse is also true—ergonomics can support the achievement of company success. Mark Middlesworth, founder of Ergonomics Plus Inc., identifies the five proven benefits of a strong workplace ergonomics process: (1) ergonomics reduces costs, (2) ergonomics improves productivity, (3) ergonomics improves quality, (4) ergonomics improves employee engagement, and (5) ergonomics creates a better safety culture (Middlesworth 2016).

Since ergonomics (and its synonym human factors), by definition, includes the objectives of improved system performance and operator well-being, everyone has something to gain in the application of human factors knowledge. Globally, the problem of work-related ill health costs about 4% of the World's GDP (WHO 2009). For companies, the costs of poor ergonomics are usually reckoned in terms of sickness–absenteeism costs, although the "hidden" or indirect costs in terms of increased quality deficits, poorer organizational performance, hiring and replacement costs, reduced productivity, and so on can cost many times the direct costs of any injury (Neumann 2007). "Good ergonomics is good economics" (Hendrick 1996).

5.1   The evolution of ergonomics

In 2000, the International Ergonomics Association (IEA) defined ergonomics as "the scientific discipline that analyzes the effect of interactions between humans and their surroundings in order to optimize human well-being and overall system performance" (IEA Council 2000). The first evidence of ergonomics was found in Egypt and Greece where they started building tools, equipment, and workplaces illustrating ergonomic principles, which were considered modern or advanced at that time. Therefore, basic ergonomics has existed since humans started building tools to make tasks easier. A good example can be found in the description Hippocrates gave of how a surgeon's workplace should be designed and how the tools should be arranged (Ergosource 2013).

Bernardino Ramazinni (1633–1714) described work-related complaints that he saw in medical practice in the 1713 supplement to his 1700 publication titled *Diseases of Workers*. Wojciech Jastrzebowski defined ergonomics in 1857 as "based upon the truths drawn from the Science of Nature" (Ergoweb 2016).

In the early 1900s, production was highly dependable on human power and ergonomics played a key role in improving employees' productivity. ergonomics emerged in the 1940s as a scientific discipline as a consequence of the increasing complexity of technical equipment. Workers were unable to optimize the use of the machinery since they could not understand and use the equipment to its full potential (Chartered Institute of Ergonomics & Human Factors [CIEHF] 2016).

Frederick W. Taylor was a pioneer in evaluating jobs and determining the "One Best Way" they could be performed. Taylor drastically increased worker production and wages in a shoveling task by matching the shovel task with the type of material moved (ashes, coal, etc.) at Bethlehem Steel.

Frank and Lillian Gilbreth made jobs more efficient and less fatiguing through time motion analysis and standardizing tools, materials, and processes. In the 1900s, Frank and Lillian Gilbreth further expanded Taylor's methods and came up with "Time and Motion Studies." The Gilbreths looked at the different techniques that would help reduce the amount of unnecessary motions required to perform a task. For example, they studied "bricklaying" and helped reduce the number of motions required and actually increased productivity from 120 up to 350 bricks per hour. Ergonomics as a discipline had clearly found its footing (Scribd 2016).

World War II led to a great interest in human–machine interaction due to poor or confusing designs that jeopardize the efficiency of military equipment. Design concepts of fitting the machine to the size of the soldier and logical control buttons evolved (Ergoweb 2016).

However, the term ergonomics was not coined until shortly after World War II when a group of British naval scientists used it to describe the anatomical, physiological, and psychological knowledge. It started then to be applied to humans and their relationship to their work environments.

The Information Age era has led to the field of human–computer interaction (HCI). In 1957, the Human Factors and Ergonomics Society (HFES) was founded with the mission of promoting the discovery and exchange of knowledge concerning the characteristics of human beings that are applicable to the design of systems and devices of all kinds. Soon after, the IEA held its first meeting in 1961, and is now a federation of ergonomics and human factors societies from around the world. The IEA's mission is to elaborate and advance the ergonomics science and practice, and to improve the quality of life by expanding its scope of application and contribution to society (IEA 2016).

Although the early focus of ergonomics was on work environment, the importance of ergonomics has become increasingly recognized in many spheres, including the design of consumer products using User Center Design (CIEHF 2016).

Since then, concerns over workplace injuries and productivity levels have led to the development of ergonomics as a scientific discipline. Nowadays, there are 33 ergonomic societies throughout the world, including organizations in many countries such as Japan, Germany, China, and India (Leamon 2016).

5.2   The history of safety

Efforts to improve public safety date from the early era of industrialization. In the 1840s, states established railroad regulatory commissions. The power of the commissions was limited and had little influence on working conditions.

In 1908, Congress passed a federal employers' liability law that applied to railroad workers in interstate commerce. Worker fatalities that had once cost the railroads perhaps $200 now cost $2000. Two years later in 1910 and influenced by Europe, New York became the first state to pass a workmen's compensation law. Instead of requiring injured workers to sue for damages in court and prove that the employer was negligent, the new law automatically compensated all injuries at a fixed rate. Compensation became popular among businesses leaders because it made costs more predictable. To reformers and unions, it promised greater and more certain benefits. Samuel Gompers, leader of the American Federation of Labor, had studied the effects of compensation in Germany and was impressed by how it stimulated business interest in safety. Between 1911 and 1921, 44 states passed compensation laws. During the years between World War I and World War II, the combination of higher accident costs along with the institutionalization of safety concerns in large firms began to show results. Fatality among employees rates declined steadily after 1910 in some large companies and railroad employees.

The American Society of Safety Engineers (ASSE) was founded in October 14, 1911 in New York City as the United Association of Casualty Inspectors with 62 members soon after the tragic fire that occurred on March 25, 1911, when 146 garment workers died in the Triangle Shirtwaist Factory fire in New York City. ASSE is the oldest professional safety society and represents more than 37,000 practitioners committed to protecting people, property, and the environment. ASSE is at the forefront of safety engineering, design, standards development, management, and education in virtually every industry, governmental agency, labor, and in institutions of higher education. Currently, ASSE has members in over 80 countries around the globe. In addition, ASSE is the secretariat for 11 ANSI committees responsible for more than 100 occupational safety and health standards. ASSE members also serve on over 40 safety and health standards committees including three with the International Organization for Standardization (ISO) (ASSE 2016).

The first Safety Congress was held in 1912 and the National Safety Council (NSC) was founded in 1913 to pool information. Government agencies such as the Bureau of Mines and National Bureau of Standards provided scientific support while universities also researched safety problems for firms and industries. The first basic labor standards and worker benefits resulted in 1934–1936 when the Bureau of Labor Standards and Congress approved the Public Contracts Act and the Social Security Act. This led to setting the minimum working age or the minimum wage. In April 28, 1971, the Occupational Safety and Health Administration (OSHA) was established after an OSH Act of 1970 to ensure safe and healthful working conditions for workers by setting and enforcing standards and by providing training, outreach, education, and assistance. OSHA estimates that the rate of reported serious workplace injuries and illnesses has declined from 11% in 1972 to 3.6% in 2009 (NSC 2016).

After World War II, newly powerful labor unions played an increasingly important role in work safety. In the 1960s, however, economic expansion again led to rising injury rates and the resulting political pressures led Congress to establish the OSHA and the Mine Safety and Health Administration in 1970. The work of these agencies had been controversial, but on balance they have contributed to the continuing reductions in work injuries since 1970 (Economic History Association [EH.net] copyright 2016).

Since 1971, OSHA and its state partners have coupled with employers, safety and health professionals, unions, and advocates. They have had a dramatic effect on workplace safety since fatality and injury rates have dropped significantly. It is estimated that in 1970 around 14,000 workers were killed on the job.

In 1989, OSHA Voluntary safety and Health Program Management Guidelines set expectations for company safety and health programs based on the degree of employee participation in the following elements:

• Development of the program including conducting training and education
• Workplace audits including collecting data
• Program interviews
• The authority to stop activities when deemed hazardous Society of Manufacturing Engineers (SME) it is estimated that 1998.

While in 1970 around 14,000 workers were killed on the job (estimation), the number fell to approximately 4340 in 2009. At the same time, U.S. employment has almost doubled and now includes over 130 million workers at more than 7.2 million worksites. Since the passage of the OSH Act, the rate of reported serious workplace injuries and illnesses has declined from 11% of workers in 1972 to 3.6% of workers in 2009. OSHA safety and health standards, including those for trenching, machine guarding, asbestos, benzene, lead, and bloodborne pathogens, have prevented countless work-related injuries, illnesses, and deaths (OSHA 2016).

5.3 Human factors: Ergonomics and safety

There are several domains of specialization within the Human Factors and ergonomics field. Physical ergonomics is concerned with human anatomy and anthropometric, physiological, and biomechanical characteristics as they relate to physical activity of the worker. This area of ergonomics identifies physical disorders, such as arthritis or carpal tunnel syndrome. One of the most prevalent types of work-related injuries is musculoskeletal disorder. Every year 1.8 million U.S. workers experience work-related musculoskeletal disorders (WRMDs), and nearly 600,000 of the injuries are serious enough to cause workers to miss work (Jeffress 2000).

Cognitive ergonomics is concerned with the mental workload of performing a task or carrying a job. This area of ergonomics focuses on the interactions among humans and other elements of the workplace. That includes work stress, human reliability, memory, reasoning, and decision-making as these may relate to human–system interaction and HCI.

Organizational ergonomics tackles the optimization of socio-technical systems, which includes organizational structures, policies, communication, staff resource management, work design, work schedule, work systems, teamwork, new work programs, training, virtual organizations, telework, etc.

As defined by the World Health Organization, occupational safety and health deals with all aspects of health and safety in the workplace and has a strong focus on primary prevention of hazards. It is a multidisciplinary field concerned with the safety, health, and welfare of humans at the workplace. The promotion of safety at work is concerned with preventing harm from any incidental hazards arising in the workplace. Research suggests that human error contributes to unsafe practices and accidents more than two-thirds of the time in industries such as manufacturing (Wilson-Donnelly et al. 2005).

A major American standards organization is the American National Standards Institute (ANSI). Usually, members of a particular industry voluntarily serve in a committee to study safety issues and propose standards. Experts recommend standards to ANSI, which reviews and adopts them. Many government regulations require that products sold or used must comply with a particular ANSI standard.

Ludwig et al. developed an integrated risk management model to measure the effective management of productivity, quality, risk, and safety and how to drive manufacturing profitability and sustainability. They stated, "with the ability to identify the failure and solve problems quickly, we have dramatically increased productivity by reducing up to 70% of the safety breakdown time" (Ludwig et al. 2011).

However, the practice of *Safety* also brings financial benefits to the table. A safe work environment impacts a project's bottom line both directly and indirectly. Costs associated with incidents, including lost costs, worker's comp claims, insurance costs, and legal fees, are minimized in a safe work environment. So are the indirect costs that follow incidents, including the lost productivity that occurs when people turn their attention to dealing with an incident. Effective safety means fewer schedule interruptions, which minimize operating costs.

On the flip side, a safe work environment boosts employee morale, which, in turn, increases productivity, efficiency, and profit. When employees feel like they have a safe work environment, they can accomplish their full potential. There are fewer staff absences, less turnover and an improvement in the quality of work (Robinson 2015).

5.4   Ergonomics and safety tools

When it comes to ergonomics, organizational leaders need to decide if they want to consider participatory ergonomics. Organizations can have ergonomics programs without being participatory. In order to implement participatory ergonomics in a facility, an assessment of management, social, and cultural aspects of the employees is required (SME 1998). If the assessment leads to acceptance from management and it looks viable from the social and cultural standpoint of view, then it is worth it to implement it and the benefits will be worth it in the long term. Just like any effort, employees at all levels in the enterprise must buy in and be completely onboard and trained in order for the effort to succeed.

The Washington State Department of Labor and Industries has industry guidelines that have been generated by business associations, labor groups, and governmental agencies to prevent injuries. Depending on the manufacturing type, a set of best practices, handbooks, and manuals are provided.

Ergonomics and safety is usually measured in manufacturing companies as a stand-alone area instead, integrating it as a core function of the manufacturing enterprise. Preventive ergonomics tools assist in continuously improving the employees' tasks and are key to reduce the risk of injuries and accidents. Risk assessment methods such as screening tools help in identifying potential risks and contributing factors. Workers or employees in charge of using these tools must be trained on how to collect and analyze data properly. The analysis of hazards and risk and their reduction also supports improvements in quality, productivity, and efficiency. In fact, very often manufacturing organizations measure ergonomics along with quality and terms such as Kaizen are no longer just used in quality departments. A lot of ergonomics and safety initiatives in manufacturing organizations have been implemented along with TQM efforts. Occupational safety and health needs to be considered just like quality, a continuous improvement area (SME 1998). Ferreras and Crumpton-Young (2005) presented at the eighth annual applied ergonomics conference "How to Control an ergonomics Program through Six-Sigma Methodology."

Checklists are also greatly used in job–site analysis since these tools allow us to review quickly a lot of risk, hazards, and potential issues that can lead to an accident or injury. In addition, employee surveys and comments or narratives also help in reducing risks and eliminating hazards. Furthermore, injury and illness record analysis also provide an opportunity to capture and analyze the issue in greater detail.

Finally, the following tools have also become very popular among ergonomists: National Institute for Occupational Safety and Health (NIOSH) lifting equation, rapid entire body assessment (REBA), rapid upper limb assessment (RULA), snook tables, hand–arm vibration, and Washington Industrial Safety and Health Act (WISHA) lifting calculator, among others.

5.5   A holistic ergonomics and safety model

After performing an extended literature review in ergonomics and safety, no deterministic model was found to evaluate and combine these components. Equation 5.1 represents a new ergonomics and safety index model developed to evaluate the ergonomics and safety success of manufacturing organizations. Additive mathematical operands are used to group the ergonomics and safety MFs obtained per factor variable.

$$ES(Plant,\ Year) = (W_{RC} \times RC) + (W_{LWDC} \times LWDC) + (W_{OSHA} \times OSHA)$$
$$+ (W_{II} \times II) + (W_{PE} \times PE) + (W_{WC} \times WC) \tag{5.1}$$

where:
  ES = Ergonomics and safety value per plant per year
  W_{RC} = weight *of replacement cost*
  RC = *replacement cost* degree of membership
  W_{LWDC} = weight of *lost workday cases*
  $LWDC$ = *lost workday cases* degree of membership
  W_{OSHA} = weight of *OSHA fines*
  $OSHA$ = *OSHA fines* degree of membership
  W_{II} = weight of *OSHA injury and illness*
  II = *OSHA injury and illness* degree of membership
  W_{PE} = weight of *proactive ergonomics*
  PE = *proactive ergonomics* degree of membership
  W_{WC} = weight of *workers' compensation*
  WC = *workers' compensation* degree of membership

The ergonomics and safety index model includes a great variety of factor variables, such as annual replacement costs (extra wages generated by an injury, illness, or accident), lost workday cases, OSHA fines, OSHA recordable cases, workers' compensation expenses, and proactive ergonomics activities. Additive mathematical operands were applied to combine all the ergonomics and safety MFs and develop a mathematical model. The following section includes the weights obtained from SMEs, which will be key in the development of an ergonomics and safety Fuzzy model.

5.6 Weights

The weights for every factor variable identified in the Fuzzy model were obtained from SMEs in the industry and academia. Through a pairwise comparison, weights are calculated. Figure 5.1 illustrates the ergonomics and safety weights obtained from the Analytical Hierarchy Process performed through Expert Choice.

The ergonomics and safety inconsistency ratio was evaluated (0.02), which is smaller than 0.1. Therefore, the ratio obtained reflects coherent judgments and opinions given by SME. Work wages in Figure 5.1 represent the replacement cost generated after an injury due to lost workdays and wages.

Table 5.1 provides the performance measures and metrics to assess the ergonomics and safety index model. For example, replacement cost reflects the cost that takes place after an injury, due to lost days and work wages. In addition, proactive ergonomics includes costs, such as

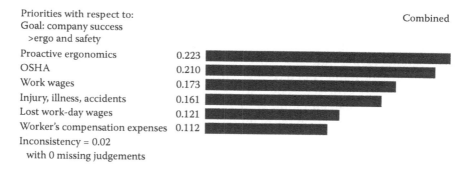

Figure 5.1 Ergonomics and safety index model weights.

Table 5.1 Ergonomics and safety performance measures and metrics

Performance measures	Metrics
Lost workday cases	Lost workday rate (frequency)
Employee replacement cost	Employee replacement cost (lost workdays × wages)
OSHA fines	OSHA fines (dollars)
OSHA injury and illness rate	OSHA recordable incidence rate
Proactive ergonomics	Cost of an ergonomics program
Workers' compensation expenses	Cost per hour worked

awareness training, ergonomics assessments, or cost to maintain an ergonomics program.

5.7   Case example

As a typical manufacturing leader, Pam Rogers cares about her employees and customers' safety. However, she does not see the economic value of improving and investing in ergonomics. While she gets notified every time a worker's compensation case or major accident or injury arises, Pam does not have a systematic approach to measure ergonomics and safety. The following section shows the data collection and MF developed to implement a new ergonomics and safety index model in Pam's firm.

5.7.1   Data collection and membership function development

An MF per ergonomics and safety factor variable was developed to appropriately develop a complex and holistic model. The first MF to be presented is replacement cost.

The *replacement cost* generated after an accident, injury, or illness is estimated by multiplying the median lost workdays by the salary rate of the manufacturing industry. Since no scale was found within the literature review, the number of days away from work published by the Bureau of Labor Statistics (BLS) was used to develop a replacement cost scale. The historical data obtained represent the median days away from work and the standard hourly rate in the manufacturing industry from 1994 to 2006. Median days away from work from the BLS is the measure used to summarize the varying lengths of absences from work among the cases with days away from work. Table 5.2 includes all the historical data obtained from the manufacturing industry to develop the replacement cost or X-axis, and the degree of membership or Y-axis (BLS 2007).

A sigmoidal MF is selected to represent the replacement cost factor variable. Figure 5.2 represents the replacement cost MF obtained from plotting the amount in dollars within the X-axis and the degree of membership within the Y-axis (BLS 2007). When the cost is $1650, the degree of membership is 0 so it does not belong in the set of values represented in the function; however, a $481 cost fully belongs to the MF since the degree of membership is 1.

The second MF to be presented in this chapter is lost workday cases. *Lost workday cases* are represented by the lost workday rate, which is calculated by multiplying the total number of lost workdays for the year by 200,000, and the result is then divided by the number of employee labor hours at the organization. Since no scale was found within the literature review, the number of cases with days away from work, job transfer,

Table 5.2 Replacement cost membership function values for the manufacturing industry

Year	Days away from work	Average salary/day ($)	X—Replacement cost ($)	Y—Degree of membership
1994	5	96.32	481.60	1.00
1995	5	98.72	493.60	1.00
1996	5	102	510.00	1.00
1997	5	105.12	525.60	1.00
1998	7	107.6	753.20	0.90
1999	8	110.8	886.40	0.77
2000	8	114.56	916.48	0.74
2001	10	118.08	1180.80	0.35
2002	12	122.32	1467.84	0.06
2003	13	125.92	1636.96	0.00
2004	13	129.2	1679.60	0.00
2005	11	132.48	1457.28	0.07
2006	11	134.4	1478.40	0.06

Source: BLS. 2007. Median days away from work. http://www.bls.gov

or restriction published by the BLS was used to develop a lost workday cases scale. The historical data obtained represent the nonfatal occupational injury and illness incidence rates per 100 full-time workers in the manufacturing industry from 1992 to 2005. Table 5.3 includes all the historical data obtained from the manufacturing industry to develop the lost workday cases or X-axis, and the degree of membership or Y-axis (BLS* 2006).

A sigmoidal MF is selected to represent the lost workday cases factor variable; Figure 5.3 represents the lost workday cases MF obtained from plotting the frequency rate within the X-axis and the degrees of

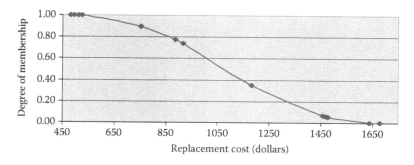

Figure 5.2 Replacement cost membership function.

Table 5.3 Lost workday cases (frequency rate) membership function values for the manufacturing industry

Year	X—No. of cases away from work	Y—Degree of membership
1992	5.4	0
1993	5.3	0.02
1994	5.5	0
1995	5.3	0.02
1996	4.9	0.18
1997	4.8	0.25
1998	4.7	0.32
1999	4.6	0.41
2000	4.5	0.5
2001	4.1	0.82
2002	4.1	0.82
2003	3.8	0.96
2004	3.6	1
2005	3.5	1

Source: BLS*. 2006. Lost workday cases. http://wwwbls.gov/iif/oshsum.htm

membership within the Y-axis. The graph shows that when the frequency rate is 5.5, the degree of membership is 0 so it verily belongs to the function; however, a 3.5 frequency rate fully belongs to the MF since the degree of membership is 1.

The third MF to be presented is *OSHA fines*. Since no scale was found within the literature review, the OSHA penalties adjusted were used to develop an OSHA fines scale. The MF presented uses OSHA penalties due

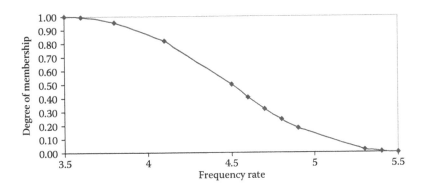

Figure 5.3 Lost workday cases membership function.

to violations to estimate the degree of membership. OSHA provides penalty reductions based on the size of the employer and other factors. States that operate their own occupational safety and health plans are required to adopt maximum penalty levels that are at least as effective as those of Federal OSHA. OSHA offers a variety of options for employers looking for compliance assistance (OSHA 2007).

A sigmoidal MF is selected to represent the OSHA fines factor variable; Figure 5.4 represents the MF developed from plotting the amount of fines in dollars within the X-axis, and the degree of membership within the Y-axis. The graph shows that when the cost is $72,500, the degree of membership is 0, so it barely belongs to the function; however, a $0 cost fully belongs to the MF since the degree of membership is 1.

The fourth MF presented in this chapter is *OSHA injury and illness.* The OSHA injury and illness MF is developed using the incident rate which is calculated by multiplying the number of recordable cases by 200,000; the result is then divided by the number of labor hours at the organization. Since no scale was found within the literature review, the nonfatal occupational injury and illness incidence rates per 100 full-time workers published by the BLS was used to develop the OSHA injury and illness scale. The historical data obtained represent the nonfatal occupational injury and illness incidence rates per 100 full-time workers in the manufacturing sector from 1992 to 2005. Table 5.4 represents the numeric values obtained from the MF, which is represented by a sigmoidal shape in Figure 5.5. Table 5.4 includes the year, national illness, and incidence rates or X-value, and the degree of membership or Y-value.

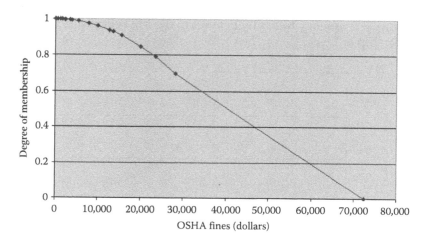

Figure 5.4 OSHA fines membership function.

Table 5.4 OSHA injury and illness membership function values for the manufacturing industry

Year	X—OSHA injury and illness rate	Y—Degree of membership
1992	12.5	0
1993	12.1	0.01
1994	12.2	0
1995	11.6	0.04
1996	10.6	0.19
1997	10.3	0.25
1998	9.7	0.41
1999	9.2	0.56
2000	9	0.62
2001	8.1	0.83
2002	7.2	0.96
2003	6.8	0.99
2004	6.6	1
2005	6.3	1

Source: BLS. 2006. Nonfatal occupational injury and illness incidence rates per 100 full-time workers by industry division. http://www.bls.gov

A sigmoidal MF was selected to represent the OSHA injury and illness rate. Figure 5.5 shows the OSHA recordable incidence rate MF, which represents the manufacturing industry historical data obtained from the BLS. The graph shows that, when the frequency rate is 12.5, the degree of membership is 0, so it barely belongs to the function; however, the 6.3 frequency rate fully belongs to the MF because the degree of membership is 1.

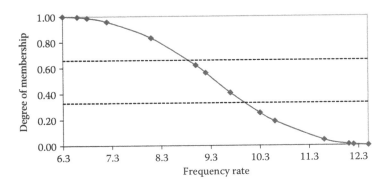

Figure 5.5 OSHA injury and illness membership function.

The fifth MF presented in this chapter is *proactive ergonomics*. Many activities can be identified and considered as proactive in ergonomics and safety, but most important is the development and support of an ergonomics and safety program. It can be measured by the cost of maintaining such a program in place. The National Institute for Occupational Safety and Health (NIOSH) (1997) published a report titled *Elements of Ergonomics Programs: A Primer Based on Workplace Evaluations of Musculoskeletal Disorders*, which identifies the key elements of an ergonomics program. The following elements are critical in the development and sustainability of a successful ergonomics program.

1. Management commitment and supervision
2. Worksite analysis
3. Injury prevention or control
4. Injury management
5. Training and education

To develop the proactive ergonomics MF, the cost of developing and supporting a full ergonomics program was used. Several subject matter experts from academia and industry were interviewed, and a minimum and maximum cost of developing and maintaining an ergonomics and safety program within a manufacturing plant of 250–500 employees was developed. Figure 5.6 shows a sigmoidal MF, which represents proactive ergonomics. When the cost is $10,000, the degree of membership is 0, so it barely belongs to the function; however, the $23,000 cost fully belongs to the MF because the degree of membership is 1.

The BLS report on Employer Costs for Employee Compensation provides national data and historical averages that assist in the development of an MF. The historical data obtained represent the annual values of the manufacturing industry from 1986 to 2006 (BLS* 2007).

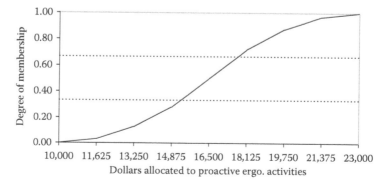

Figure 5.6 Proactive ergonomics membership function.

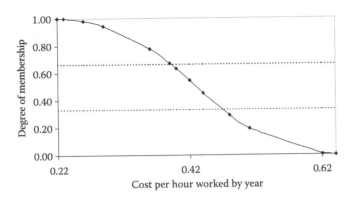

Figure 5.7 Workers' compensation membership function.

A sigmoidal MF represents the workers' compensation factor variable. Figure 5.7 represents the workers' compensation MF for the manufacturing industry. The X-axis represents the employer costs per hour worked for employee workers' compensation, and the Y-axis represents the degree of membership obtained. The following graph shows that when the cost per hour is $0.62, the degree of membership is 0, so it barely belongs to the function; however, $0.22 cost per hour fully belongs to the MF because the degree of membership is 1.

The following section focuses on the ergonomics and safety model implementation in Pam's manufacturing plants (A and B). It also discusses where Pam's plants fit within the MFs developed using the manufacturing industry scales and averages.

5.7.2   Ergonomics and safety index model results

The ergonomics and safety program in Plant A had several types of reports such as the OSHA compliance reports, as well as insurance carrier reports showing workers' compensation expenses. Historical data were successfully identified for the ergonomics and safety model; however, several key performance measures had not been traditionally measured or fully documented, such as proactive ergonomics activities.

Tables 5.5 and 5.6 summarize the data obtained from Plant A (Figure 5.5) and Plant B (Figure 5.6). Tools such as checklists, safety records, and production reports were used to evaluate ergonomics and safety measures. These data were used to validate the ergonomics and safety MFs developed using the manufacturing industry scales or historical behavior. Both plants are at a similar level of performance, with the exception that Plant B invested more than double than Plant A in proactive ergonomics.

Table 5.5 Ergonomics and safety data from Plant A

Factor variable	2002	2003	2004	2005
Replacement cost	$0	$0	$0	$0
Lost workday cases	.98	1.56	2.91	2.77
OSHA fines	$0	$0	$0	$0
OSHA recordable injury and illness rate	1.95	3.1	4	4.93
Replacement machinery and damaged material	$0	$0	$0	$0
Proactive ergonomics	$10,290	$10,395	$10,490	$10,577
Workers' compensation	$0.09	$0.07	$0.06	$0.06

Table 5.7 shows the total value of all the factor variables in the ergonomics and safety model within Plant A and B. These values are obtained after fitting Plant A and Plant B in the MFs. Total value is then calculated by multiplying the degree of membership or Y-axis values by the weights obtained in Figure 5.1. Unfortunately, Pam and her safety managers never captured some data and reports that would have helped with some metrics. Once a company starts collecting data more frequently, the leaders will be able to predict the future of ergonomics and safety in their sites and the impact on the overall company success. After all the weights and degree of membership have been multiplied per variable, all the values are added as the ergonomics and safety model states. The following table represents all the values of the ergonomics and safety index model in Plant A and Plant B.

5.7.3   Ergonomics and safety index model validation

This section presents the validation process implemented to assess the accuracy of the ergonomics and safety model. The Fuzzy model developed is

Table 5.6 Ergonomics and safety data from Plant B

Factor variable	2002	2003	2004	2005	2006
Replacement cost	$0	$0	$0	$0	$0
Lost workday cases	2.96	3.83	3.91	7.45	3.28
OSHA fines	$0	$0	$0	$0	$0
OSHA recordable cases	2.96	3.83	3.91	7.45	3.28
Replacement machinery and damaged material	$0	$0	$0	$0	$5465
Proactive ergonomics	$8640	$8640	$12,047	$8640	$24,742
Workers' compensation	$0.07	$0.1	$0.25	$0.13	$0.17

Table 5.7 Ergonomics and safety model overview

Data source	Year	OSHA fines	LWDC	Replacement cost	Injury rates	Proactive Act	WC	Total
Plant A	2002	0.2100	0.1210	0.1419	0.1610	0.0002	0.1120	0.7461
Plant A	2003	0.2100	0.1210	0.1603	0.1610	0.0004	0.1120	0.7647
Plant A	2004	0.2100	0.1210	0.1727	0.1610	0.0006	0.1120	0.7773
Plant A	2005	0.2100	0.1210	0.1724	0.1610	0.0009	0.1120	0.7773
Plant B	2003	0.2100	0.1144	0.1064	0.1610	0.0000	0.1120	0.7038
Plant B	2004	0.2100	0.1108	0.0995	0.1562	0.0111	0.1109	0.6985
Plant B	2005	0.2100	0.0000	0.0467	0.1449	0.0000	0.1120	0.5136
Plant B	2006	0.2100	0.1210	0.0272	0.1610	0.2230	0.1120	0.8542

compared with a gold standard. OSHA guidelines were selected as the ergonomics gold standard while key safety practices were chosen to develop a new gold standard tool—*OSHA Ergonomics and Safety Guidelines Assessment.* The purpose of this tool is to assess if OSHA ergonomics guidelines and safety guidelines are addressed in any manufacturing organization. The assessment developed as the gold standard consists of 19 questions, 8 addressing key ergonomics factors and the other 11 related to safety factors. Table 5.8 provides the results obtained from evaluating the ergonomics and safety level using the gold standard tool on Plant A and Plant B.

Table 5.9 provides a comparison of the total values obtained from the ergonomics and safety index model versus the gold standard value in Plant A and Plant B and their respective year. *The OSHA Ergonomics and Safety Guidelines Assessment* tool provides us an opportunity to assess if key characteristics of successful ergonomics and safety programs are observed in the organization. The tool also facilitates the validation of the ergonomics and safety index model presented in this chapter.

The following table summarizes the interpreted ergonomics and safety model results based on a scale of low (0–0.33), medium (0.34–0.66), and high (0.67–1). Table 5.10 also compares the model results with the gold standard level obtained from Plant A and Plant B. This table is necessary for calculating the accuracy value within the ergonomics and safety model.

Table 5.11 shows the calculations to measure the accuracy of the ergonomics and safety model presented in this chapter. The accuracy of the ergonomics and safety index model is 87.5%.

5.8   Summary

Ergonomics and safety can contribute to the economic goals of an organization. For example, a company with user-friendly products can deliver

Table 5.8 Ergonomics and safety gold standard values for Plant A and Plant B

Ergonomics and safety assessment		
Question	Plant A	Plant B
1	1	0.25
2	1	0
3	0.75	0.25
4	1	0.75
5	1	1
6	1	0.75
7	1	1
8	1	1
9	1	1
10	1	1
11	1	1
12	1	1
13	1	1
14	1	1
15	0.75	0.75
16	0.25	0.75
17	0.75	0.75
18	0	0.75
19	0.5	0.75
Total	*0.84*	*0.78*

Table 5.9 Ergonomics and safety model values versus gold standard for Plant A and Plant B

Data source	Year	Total	Gold standard
Plant A	2002	0.7461	0.84
Plant A	2003	0.7647	0.84
Plant A	2004	0.7773	0.84
Plant A	2005	0.7773	0.84
Plant B	2003	0.7038	0.78
Plant B	2004	0.6985	0.78
Plant B	2005	0.5136	0.78
Plant B	2006	0.8542	0.78

Table 5.10 Ergonomics and safety model versus gold standard values for
Plant A and Plant B

Location	Year	Ergo. and safety model	Gold standard
Plant A	2002	High	High
Plant A	2003	High	High
Plant A	2004	High	High
Plant A	2005	High	High
Plant B	2003	High	High
Plant B	2004	High	High
Plant B	2005	Medium	High
Plant B	2006	High	High

Table 5.11 Accuracy values of ergonomics and safety model

Gold standard (ergonomics and safety assessment)				
Ergonomics and safety model		True	False	
	Positive	TP = 7	FP = 0	$7/(7+0) = 100\%$
	Negative	FN = 1	TN = 0	$0/(1+0) = 0$
				Accuracy $7/8 = 87.5\%$

benefits to its customers by exceeding competitors products. Furthermore, a company with human-friendly production processes can increase labor productivity and consequently reach important cost reductions. The growing consciousness of the importance of humans (customers and workers) for the success of organizations implies that ergonomics and safety have a strategic value for the management of organizations (Dul 2005).

This chapter presented a new ergonomics and safety index model that can be integrated in the organizational decision-making and design processes of any manufacturing organization. The business benefits are many and the ability to optimize human systems in organizational performance is key to lead any market. This new ergonomics and safety model provides an easy approach to measure the success of human factors characteristics in the workplace environment. This model can be used in other sectors besides manufacturing.

References

Axelsson, J. R. C. 2000. *Quality and Ergonomics: Towards Successful Integration.* Linköping studies in science andtechnology. Dissertation no. 616, University of Linköping.

BLS. 2006. Nonfatal occupational injury and illness incidence rates per 100 full-time workers by industry division. http://www.bls.gov

BLS*. 2006. Lost workday cases. http://www.bls.gov/iif/oshsum.htm

BLS. 2007. Median days away from work. http://www.bls.gov

BLS*. 2007. Employer costs per hour worked for employee compensation and costs as a percent of total compensation. http://www.bls.gov

Chartered Institute of Ergonomics & Human Factors (CIEHF). 2016. Human factors in manufacturing. Bringing safety and efficiency to manufacturing processes. Accessed October 10, 2016. http://www.ergonomics.org.uk/about-us/history/; http://www.ergonomics.org.uk/manufacturing/

Cooper, S. 2012. Make more money by making your employees happy. Forbes, Entrepreneurs. July 30, http://www.forbes.com/sites/stevecooper/2012/07/30/make-more-money-by-making-your-employees-happy/

Drury, C. G. 2000. Global quality: Linking ergonomics and production. *International Journal of Production Research*, 38(17), 4007–4008.

Dul, J. 2005. *The Strategic Value of Ergonomics for Companies*. Industrial Organization 0501006, EconWPA.

Dul, J. and W. P. Neumann. 2008. Ergonomics contributions to company strategies. *ERIM Report Series Reference No. ERS-2008-058-LIS*. SSRN. November 9, https://ssrn.com/abstract=1268578

Economic History Association (EH.net). Copyright 2016. *History of Workplace Safety in the United States*, 1880–1970. Accessed October 1, 2016. http://eh.net/encyclopedia/history-of-workplace-safety-in-the-united-states-1880-1970/

Ergosource. 2013. http://ergosource.com/articles-on-ergonomics/the-history-of-ergonomics/

Ergoweb, Inc. 2016. https://ergoweb.com/knowledge/ergonomics-101/history/

Ferreras, A. and L. Crumpton-Young. 2005. How to control an ergonomics program through Six-Sigma methodology. *Eighth Annual Applied Ergonomics Conference*, New Orleans, LA.

Hendrick, H. W. 1996. *Good Ergonomics is Good Economics*. HFES Presidential Address.

International Ergonomics Association (IEA). 2016. http://www.sjsu.edu/hfe/about/

IEA Council. 2000. *The Discipline of Ergonomics*. International Ergonomics Society, 1p.

Jeffress, C. N. 2000. *BEACON Biodynamics and Ergonomics Symposium*. University of Connecticut, Farmington, CT. October 27.

Leamon, T. B. 2016. The evolution of ergonomics. *Risk Management Magazine*. https://www.questia.com/magazine/1G1-17437209/the-evolution-of-ergonomics

Ludwig, S., Beyer, C., and R. Mauerman. 2011. Improving manufacturing safety and performance using an integrated risk management model. *Copyright 2011 Zurich American Insurance Company*.

Middlesworth, M. 2016. *5 Proven Benefits of Ergonomics in the Workplace*. Ergonomics Plus Inc. March 21, http://ergo-plus.com/workplace-ergonomics-benefits/

National Safety Council (NSC). *A History of the Safety Movement*. Accessed October 1, 2016. http://viewer.zmags.com/publication/89ffce6b#/89ffce6b/16

National Institute for Occupational Safety and Health (NIOSH). 1997. *Elements of Ergonomics Programs*. A Primer on Workplace Evaluations of Musculoskeletal Disorders. NIOSH Publication No. 97–117. March.

Neumann, W. P. 2007. Beta v2.0.0—Available at http://www.ryerson.ca/hfe/-Ryerson University. *Inventory of Human Factors Tools and Methods*. A Work-System Design Perspective. http://www.ryerson.ca/hfe/documents/hf-tools-beta200.pdf

Occupational Safety and Health Administration (OSHA). 2016. *United States Department of Labor*. Accessed October 1, 2016. https://www.osha.gov/osha40/timeline.html

OSHA. 2007. OSHA penalties adjusted. *United States Department of Labor.*

Robinson, A. 2015. *Manufacturing Pays Off.* Infographics Manufacturing Safety. Cerasis. March 23, 2015.

Scribd. 2016. *History of Ergonomics.* http://www.ergonomics-info.com/historyof-ergonomics.html

Society of Manufacturing Engineers (SME). 1998. In: W. Karwowski and G. Salvendy (eds.), *Ergonomics in Manufacturing: Raising Productivity through Workplace Improvement*. Dearborn, MI: SME Press.

The American Society of Safety Engineers (ASSE). *What is the American Society of Safety Engineers?* Accessed October 1, 2016. http://www.asse.org/about/history/

Wilson-Donnelly, K. A., Priest, H. A., Salas, E., and C. S. Burke. 2005. The impact of organizational practices on safety in manufacturing: A review and reappraisal. *Human Factors and Ergonomics in Manufacturing & Service Industries*, 15(2), 133–176.

World Health Organization (WHO). 2009. *Who Guide to Identifying the Economic Consequences of Disease and Injury.* ISBN 978 92 4 159829 3.

Yeow, P. H. P. and R. N. Sen. 2003. Quality, productivity, occupational health and safety and cost effectiveness of ergonomics improvements in the test workstations of an electronic factory. *International Journal of Industrial Ergonomics*, 32(2), 147–163.

chapter six

Profit, productivity, and efficiency within company success

6.1 The evolution of financial measures in manufacturing organizations

As described in Chapters 1 and 2, organizational leaders have traditionally made decisions mostly based on financial measures. Nevertheless,
this type of performance measures requires great understanding to avoid
any misunderstanding. Only when sales equal production (all units manufactured are sold), manufacturing costs (materials used, direct labor
incurred, and manufacturing overhead incurred) and manufacturing
expenses (cost of goods sold) are equal (Microbuspub 2016). Traditionally,
manufacturing businesses have measured financial measures using cost
accounting. Since cost accounting systems are not subject to rules and
standards like generally accepted accounting principles (GAAP), there is
a great variety of cost accounting systems observed among companies
and even within the same enterprise (Wikipedia 2016). A limited understanding of cost accounting may cause financial statements to be incor-
rectly prepared and/or inadequately understood. Nowadays, there are
a lot of accounting tools in manufacturing that assist company leaders
in analyzing many variables and a large amount of data. These systems
provide business leaders with a greater understanding of their operating
costs associated with manufacturing their goods. For example, the IQMS
Manufacturing Accounting and Financial Management tool includes
accounts receivable, accounts payable, business intelligence, electronic
data interchange (EDI), expense tracking and reporting, financial reporting of fixed assets, general ledger, human resources and payroll, job and
process costing, invoicing, and purchasing. Consumers consider IQMS,
SAP Business One, WorkWise ERP, OmegaCube ERP, Oracle JD Edwards
Manufacturing, MIE Trak PRO, SAS Manufacturing, and E2 Shop System
the best manufacturing accounting software tools available in the market.

Since global competitiveness continues to put greater pressure on
what type of information is collected and analyzed in manufacturing
businesses, information systems have become a backbone tool or approach

for organizational leaders. Business managers rely heavily on their information systems in order to make decisions that involved operations. In almost every sector, information systems play a prominent role in regular operations that involve many functions, such as inventory levels, production schedule, material purchase, and resource planning systems, among others (MIT Press 2016). The new marketplace calls for manufacturing information systems that are lean, agile, flexible, and managed for quality (University of Missouri-St. Louis [UMSL] 2016).

6.2   *Measuring profit*

Profit is very well known as revenue minus expenses. In other words, profit is reflected in the reduction in liabilities, increase in assets, and/ or increase in owners' equity. Its absence may result in the extinction of a company. The best manufacturing performers are voracious consumers of performance data in order to predict outcomes and gain insight of the firm. While all experts agree that financial measures are essential to measure and predict company success, they do not agree on the specific financial measures.

In order to fit profit as part of the company success model, an MF for profit is presented based on historical data obtained through the net income after tax average of U.S. manufacturing corporations based on the quarterly financial report for manufacturing, mining, and trade corporations from the U.S. Department of Commerce (U.S. Census Bureau 2016a,b). The industry average or X-values and the corresponding degree of membership or Y-values necessary to develop profit MF are included. Equation 6.1 illustrates that the profit MF is commonly defined mathematically as revenue minus expenses.

$$Profit \ (Plant, Year) = Revenue - Expenses \qquad (6.1)$$

where:
   Profit (Plant, Year) = *Profit* MF
   Revenue = sales (annually) or assets
   Expenses = factors, such as labor, material, variable overhead, fixed overhead, variable cost, income tax, legal fees, and R&D (Research and development) expenses (annually).

6.3   *Profit weight*

All the key components defined as part of the company success model have a weight. Using AHP, the weight was calculated. Profit's weight is considered by all experts, independently of their sector, the most important

Priorities with respect to:
Goal: company success

Profit   0.334

Inconsistency = 0.03

with 0 missing judgements

Figure 6.1 Profit weight.

component of company success. Profit has the largest weight (0.334), so it represents 33.4% of the total weight of the company success model as shown in Figure 6.1. The closest weight to profit is productivity, which represents 0.163 or 16.3% of the overall model. The inconsistency ratio is 0.03, which is less than 0.1. This validates that the weight is appropriate and experts are consistent with their values.

The characterization of profit is presented in Table 6.1, which includes the performance measures and metrics identified under revenue and expenses. Revenues might be generated by operating income and nonoperating income. The following characterization considers manufacturing plants as Profit Centers.

A metric has been identified per performance measure, and the following list provides a greater understanding of each metric.

- Sales—Net sales (production revenue generated by units produced and parts sold)
- Labor—Wages of direct labor
- Material—Material cost of raw material, excluding parts, containers, and supplies
- Variable overhead—Variable expenses of a business which cannot be attributed to any specific business activity, but are still necessary for the business to function. For example, temporary workers' wages are included within this category
- Fixed overhead cost—Fixed expenses of an organization that cannot be attributed to any specific business activity, but are necessary for the business to function
- Variable cost—A cost that varies as the production level changes. Producing more adds to the variable cost and producing less reduces the variable cost
- Income taxes—State and federal income taxes
- Legal fees—Expenses allocated to legal activities or corporate premium for legal coverage
- Research and development expenditures—Cost due to research and development efforts, such as innovation, customized products, new products, and value engineering. R&D is often reported as a percent

Table 6.1 Performance measures and metrics for profit

Component	Subcomponents	Performance measures	Metrics
Profit	Revenue	Sales	Net sales (operating income)
		Capital (rent, lease, loans, etc.)	Net worth (nonoperating income)
	Expenses	Labor	Wages
		Material/ equipment	Material cost
		Capital expenses (rent, lease, loans, corporate debt, etc.)	Capital cost
		Operations (distribution, etc.)	Operations cost
		Insurance	Insurance premiums
		Depreciation	% of depreciation
		Taxes	Tax (federal, state)
		Outsource	Outsourcing cost
		Legal	Legal fees
		R&D expenditures	R&D, patent, and royalty expenses
		Employee's development/ training	Training cost
		Miscellaneous (other liabilities)	Miscellaneous cost

of revenue, so if revenue does not grow as much as planned, then R&D is reduced.

6.4   Case example on profit

Pam Rogers, as typical CEO, wants her profit to increase so she keeps a close look at the sales rate. While sales revenue has increased in the past two quarters, she does not understand why profit has not increased. She is focusing on increasing the revenue of the company, and is getting financial reports from the subsidiaries and plants quarterly. Expenses have increased, but she does not have a clear understanding what is hurting the profit so much.

6.4.1 Profit membership function

A sigmoidal MF was selected to reflect the profit component as shown in Figure 6.2. The smaller the profit amount, the lower is the degree of membership that represents the fuzzy set. The degree of membership increases as profit increases.

The lower and upper boundaries of the profit MF are \$4.29M and \$57.24M, respectively. Figure 6.2 shows that when profit is \$4.29M, the degree of membership is 0, so it barely belongs to the function; however, \$57.24M of profit fully belongs to the MF since the degree of membership is 1. Industry data from the U.S. Census Bureau (2006a,b) were used to develop MF. Table 6.2 presents all the Profit data collected from Plant A. Pam's company treats manufacturing plants as cost centers.

Table 6.3 presents summarized data obtained from Plant A such as total revenue and expenses as well as the overall annual profit of Plant A.

The profit values obtained from Plant A were plotted in the X-axis within the MF in order to identify the corresponding Y-values or the degree of membership within the fuzzy set. Revenue as well as expenses has increased in Plant A from 2002 to 2005, but profit has also increased. Table 6.4 presents the profit values or X-values and the corresponding degree of membership or Y-values within the profit MF. In addition, the total value in the last column represents the multiplication of the degree of membership by the weight obtained by the AHP method.

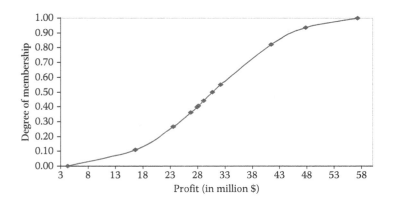

Figure 6.2 Profit MF.

Table 6.2 Profit data from Plant A

Subcomp.	Factor variable	2002	2003	2004	2005
Revenue	Sales	$89,255,457	$95,164,838	$97,210,700	$116,748,863
Expenses	Labor	$3,966,841	$4,346,313	$4,988,984	$5,785,441
	Material	$38,932,943	$40,983,172	$42,433,426	$52,058,829
	Var. O/H	$5,081,634	$5,633,951	$5,340,723	$6,306,243
	Fixed O/H	$5,571,857	$6,135,467	$5,563,287	$5,898,804
	Var. cost	$47,981,417	$50,963,436	$52,763,133	$64,150,514
	Income tax	$3,878,532	$3,736,103	$4,308,780	$5,993,600
	Legal fees	$1,650,000	$1,870,000	$2,296,000	$3,080,000
	R&D expenses	$1,652,434	$1,696,950	$1,740,909	$1,576,122

Table 6.3 Summarized *Profit* data from Plant A

Year	2002	2003	2004	2005
Revenue	$89,255,457	$95,164,838	$97,210,700	$116,748,863
Expenses	$60,734,240	$64,401,956	$66,672,109	$80,699,040
Profit	$28,521,217	$30,762,882	$30,538,591	$36,049,823

Table 6.4 *Profit* MF values for Plant A

Year	X—Profit (millions of dollars)	Y—Degree of membership	Total value
2002	28.5	0.42	0.1397
2003	30.5	0.49	0.1637
2004	30.8	0.50	0.1666
2005	36	0.68	0.2265

Table 6.5 presents all the profit data collected over Plant B. The plant is also managed as a Cost Center, so adjustments have been made in order to fit the data in the profit characterization.

Table 6.6 presents the summarized data obtained from Plant B, which includes total revenue, expenses, and the overall annual profit of Plant B. Clearly, this plant is suffering from revenue reduction and expense increase.

Table 6.7 presents the profit values or X-values and the corresponding degree of membership or Y-values within the profit MF for Plant B. In addition, the total value that represents the multiplication of the degree of membership by the weight is included in the last column.

Table 6.5 Profit data from Plant B

Subcomp.	Factor variables	2002	2003	2004	2005	2006
		Data collection sheet for factor variables of Profit				
Revenue	Sales	$87,702,081	$108,123,975	$115,634,267	$140,804,357	$107,616,354
Expenses	Labor	$5,830,646	$6,662,875	$7,865,005	$10,055,279	$9,484,963
	Material	$59,171,530	$67,151,500	$70,430,497	$90,930,194	$94,961,479
	Var. O/H	$1,221,253	$8,762,331	$9,900,780	$10,640,997	$9,895,246
	Fixed O/H	$5,480,083	$6,362,835	$5,906,512	$6,110,756	$7,881,411
	Var. cost	$72,247,292	$88,939,588	$93,826,574	$117,085,725	$122,221,000
	Income tax	$1,008,579	$615,139	$2,636,452	$5,097,067	$7,411,914
	Legal fees	$902,836	$1,334,400	$1,959,261	$2,556,348	$2,642,192
	R&D expenses	$1,809,648	$1,917,682	$2,116,946	$2,620,607	$2,289,640

Table 6.6 Summarized *Profit* data from Plant B

Year	2002	2003	2004	2005	2006
Revenue	$87,702,081	$108,123,975	$115,634,267	$140,804,357	$107,616,354
Expenses	$81,448,438	$99,169,644	$106,445,745	$133,470,503	$142,446,157
Profit	$6,253,643	$8,954,331	$9,188,522	$7,333,854	($34,829,803)

Table 6.7 *Profit* MF values for Plant B

Plant B	X—Profit (millions of dollars)	Y—Degree of membership	Total value
2002	6.3	0.02	0.0081
2003	9	0.05	0.0165
2004	9.2	0.05	0.0173
2005	7.3	0.03	0.0109
2006	−35	0	0

Profit data were mainly obtained from financial and accounting reports. In addition, tax, legal, and R&D reports provided data for factor variables, such as taxes, legal fees, and R&D expenses. Plant A had traditionally measured this component in terms of gross percentage (before corporate overhead), and in terms of performance to the plant's flex budget, since Plant A is managed as a Cost Center (based on a budget). All the historical data for profit were measured in U.S. dollars per year. Pam's manufacturing plans have traditionally measured their financial success by their ability to operate within their allocated budget. In other words, the subsidiary will monitor performance over a flexible budget. Pam's Chief Financial Officer at the headquarters forecasts annual sales, and based on that are developed annual budget projections for every plant. Operational managers must avoid exceeding the allocated budget, which leads to a limited organizational view and the ability to invest in internal continuous improvement efforts. Plant A is 5 times more profitable than Plant B, and Pam needs to make a hard decision if keeping Plant B open is worth it.

6.5   *Productivity in manufacturing organizations*

Productivity is an overall measure of the ability to produce a good or service. It is the measure of how specified resources are managed to accomplish timely objectives as stated in terms of quantity. Productivity may also be defined as an index that measures output (goods and services) relative to the input (labor, materials, energy, etc., used to produce the output). Productivity is useful as a relative measure of actual output of production compared to the actual input of resources. As output increases for a level of input, or as the amount of input decreases for a constant level of output, an increase in productivity occurs. In other words, productivity as a measure describes how well the resources of an organization are being used to produce a good. There are two major ways to increase productivity: by increasing the numerator (output) or decreasing the denominator (input). A similar effect would be seen if both input and output increased, but output increased faster than input; or if input and output decreased, but input decreased faster than output.

Company leaders and operations managers have many areas to measure productivity, such as labor productivity, machine productivity, capital productivity, energy productivity, and so on. A productivity ratio can be computed for a department, a facility, an organization, or even an entire country. For example, the United States Bureau of Labor Statistics produces national productivity statistics and related cost measures that are designed for use in economic analysis. It forecasts and analyzes changes in prices, wages, and technology. There are two primary types of productivity statistics BLS focuses on: (a) labor productivity measures output per hour of labor and (b) multifactor productivity measures output per unit of combined inputs, which consist of labor and capital, and, in some cases, intermediate inputs such as fuel (BLS 2016).

Since productivity is a relative measure, it is meaningful or useful to compare it to something. For example, businesses can compare their productivity values to that of similar firms or other departments within the same firm, or against past productivity data for the same firm or department (or even one machine). This approach allows firms to measure productivity improvement over time and/or the impact of certain decisions, such as new processes, equipment, and so on. Productivity is a required tool in evaluating and monitoring the performance of an organization, especially a manufacturing business. When directed at specific issues and problems, productivity measures can be very powerful. In essence, productivity measures are the yardsticks of effective resource use.

Proper use of productivity measures can give the plant's manager an indication of how to improve productivity: either increase the numerator of the measure, decrease the denominator, or both. Manufacturing leaders are concerned with how productivity measures relate to competitiveness and market leadership. If two firms have the same level of output, but one requires less input thanks to a higher level of productivity, that firm will be able to charge a lower price and increase its market share or charge the same price as the competitor and enjoy a larger profit margin. Productivity measures can be used to compare the firm's performance to that of the industry, compare its performance with similar firms and competitors, compare performance among different departments within the firm, or compare the performance of the firm or individual departments within the firm with historical measures. Technology has been the major reason productivity has significantly increased in the manufacturing sector in the twenty-first century. As technology advances, manufacturing companies will continue to increase their productivity (Inman 2016).

Also, production techniques have had a great impact on productivity; such is the case of JIT, the pull model in production that minimizes stock and resources, and only purchases materials, produces goods, and distributes them when required. JIT produces small and continuous batches that facilitate a smooth production. This production approach has a tremendous impact on efficiency (MindTools 2016).

U.S. manufacturers are the most productive in the world. U.S. workers are 50% more productive than workers in the next 11 leading manufacturing economies. Manufacturers understand that this productivity comes from a spirit of cooperation and mutual respect between employer and employees (National Association of Manufacturers 2016).

6.6   *Measuring productivity*

There are many performance measures or indicators in productivity such as labor productivity measured by output per worker or multifactor productivity, measured by economic growth, among others (Bureau of Labor Statistics 2016). The approach used to model productivity in this work focuses more on the Capacity Utilization of manufacturing plants, while typically the Capacity Utilization rate measures the proportion of potential economic output that is actually realized. It is calculated as (actual output)/(potential output) multiplied by 100 (Investopedia 2016). The U.S. Department of Commerce report entitled "Survey of Plant Capacity" provides the desired database on 17,000 manufacturing organizations' feedback with a 90% confidence level (U.S. Census Bureau 2016a,b). The Survey of Plant Capacity Utilization provides statistics on the rates of capacity utilization for the U.S. manufacturing and publishing sectors. The Federal Reserve Board (FRB) and the Department of Defense (DOD) cofund the survey. The survey also collects data on actual, full, and emergency production levels. The following equation was used to calculate the production MF.

$$Production\ (Plant, Year) = \frac{Production\ Volume}{\left(Production\ Volume + Backlog\right)} \qquad (6.2)$$

where:
   Production (Plant, Year) = Production MF
   Production Volume = amount of units produced
   Backlog = amount of units never built

6.7 *Productivity weight*

All the key components defined as part of the company success model have a weight. Using AHP, the weight was calculated. Productivity's weight is shown in Figure 6.3, and is the second most important component of company success with a weight of 0.163, which represents 16.3% of the total weight of the company success model. The closest weight to productivity is ergonomics and safety, which represents 0.161 or 16.1% of the overall model. The inconsistency ratio is 0.03, which is less than 0.1. This validates that the weight is appropriate and experts are consistent with their values.

The characterization of productivity is presented in Table 6.8, which includes the performance measures and metrics identified under two subcomponents of the taxonomy, output and input. A few additional indicators, on-time delivery and on-time material arrival, are not part of the MF; however, they are identified as key productivity indicators as part of the productivity taxonomy. The percentage of on-time delivery and the percentage of on-time material arrival are key measures that assist plant managers and operations leaders in making productivity improvements. Table 6.8 shows the characterization of productivity or its taxonomy.

A metric has been identified per performance measure, and the following list provides a greater understanding of all the productivity metrics:

- Production volume—Total amount of units built per year
- Delivery—Percentage of units delivered to customer on-time

Productivity   0.163

Inconsistency = 0.03

with 0 missing judgements

Figure 6.3 Productivity weight.

Table 6.8 Productivity performance measures

Component	Subcomponents	Performance measures	Metrics
Productivity	Output	Production volume	Amount of units produced
		Delivery and availability	% of On-Time Delivery
		Backlog	% of production orders not met
	Input	Suppliers	% of On-Time Material Arrival

- Backlog—Amount of orders not met
- Suppliers—Percentage of material arrival from suppliers

6.8 Case example on productivity

Pam Rogers's subsidiaries are product centered. Plant A represents a manufacturing plant that focuses on commercial products and Plant B represents a manufacturing plant that focuses on residential products. Pam Rogers, along with the Chief Operating Officer, relies on the forecasting model used at the headquarters that develops projections based on previous performance. While annual sales projections are calculated at headquarters, subsidiaries keep weekly and monthly production reports and productivity is monitored quarterly and annually.

6.8.1 Productivity membership function

Figure 6.4 illustrates that a sigmoidal MF was selected to reflect the productivity component. The smaller the productivity amount, the lower is the degree of membership that represents the fuzzy set. The degree of membership increases as productivity increases. Figure 6.4 presents the developed MF for productivity. A sigmoidal MF characterizes productivity.

Figure 6.4 shown that when the productivity percentage is 63, the degree of membership is 0, so it barely belongs to the function; however, 80% of productivity fully belongs to the MF since the degree of membership is 1.

Table 6.9 presents all the productivity data collected over Plant A, which are used to evaluate the productivity level within this subsidiary.

Even though all the data from the previous table were collected, only Production Volume and Backlog were used to calculate productivity in

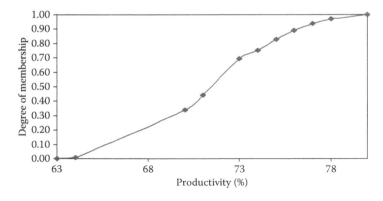

Figure 6.4 Productivity MF.

Table 6.9 Productivity data from Plant A

Subcomp.	Factor variable	2002	2003	2004	2005
Output	Production volume	43,174 units	45,805 units	49,011 units	52,740 units
	Delivery	60.3%	61.0%	61.70%	60.10%
	Backlog	6300 units	10,263 units	5334 units	8391 units
Input	Suppliers	86%	82%	80%	78%

Table 6.10 Summarized productivity data from Plant A

Year	2002	2003	2004	2005
Productivity rate	87%	82%	90%	86%

Plant A, which is illustrated in Table 6.10. While Production Volume has increased annually, backlog, on-time delivery, and on-time suppliers need an improvement. Productivity was calculated as production volume divided by the summation of the amount of units produced and the backlog (Table 6.12).

Table 6.11 presents productivity for the manufacturing industry or X-values, and degree of membership or Y-values of Plant A. The total value is based on the multiplication of degree of membership by the weight.

Table 6.12 presents all the productivity data collected over Plant B, which were used to calculate the productivity MF. Plant B has a lower (56.8%) On-Time Delivery percentage than Plant A (60.1%), but it has a significantly higher (90%) On-Time Suppliers' rate than Plant A (78%).

Even though all the data from the previous table were collected, only Production Volume and Backlog were used to calculate productivity in Plant B, which is illustrated in Table 6.13. Clearly, Plant B is performing better than Plant A when it comes to productivity. Plant B produces 6 times more units than Plant A. Plant B has agreements with its suppliers on quality and delivery standards. Both subsidiaries have a similar delivery rate, which needs to improve.

Table 6.11 Productivity MF values for Plant A

Year	X—Productivity percentage	Y—Degree of membership	Total value
2002	87	1	0.1630
2003	82	1	0.1630
2004	90	1	0.1630
2005	86	1	0.1630

Table 6.12 Productivity data from Plant B

Subcomp.	Factor variable	2003	2004	2005	2006
Output	Production volume	274,889 units	303,273 units	359,291 units	334,393 units
	Delivery	65%	65%	60.47%	56.79%
	Backlog	7752 units	22,321 units	7761 units	6855 units
Input	Suppliers	80%	85%	80%	90%

Table 6.13 Summarized productivity data from Plant B

Year	2002	2003	2004	2005
Productivity rate	97%	93%	98%	98%

Table 6.14 Productivity MF values for Plant B

Year	X—Productivity percentage	Y—Degree of membership	Total value
2003	97	1	0.1630
2004	93	1	0.1630
2005	98	1	0.1630
2006	98	1	0.1630

Table 6.14 presents the productivity percentage or X-values, degree of membership or Y-values, and the total value obtained by multiplying the degree of membership by the weight.

Production reports, as well as shipping and handling records, among other documents, were used to collect the productivity data. Pam's headquarters keep track of on-time delivery, but clearly both subsidiaries need to investigate the root cause of delivery delays and make improvements. Section 6.9, which focuses on efficiency, elaborates on some of the productivity performance measures covered in this section.

6.9   Efficiency in manufacturing organizations

Often, efficiency is confused with productivity. Efficiency is generally seen as the ratio of the time needed to perform a task to some predetermined standard time. It is outcome-oriented rather than output-oriented, which is the case with productivity (Reference for Business 2016).

Efficiency is achieved in manufacturing when resources are optimized and waste is eliminated. Waste is anything that does not add value to the end product. MindTools (2016) recommends starting by checking eight categories of waste, but there are more:

1. Overproduction—Are you producing more than consumers demand?
2. Waiting—How much lag time is there between production steps?
3. Inventory (work in progress)—Are your supply levels and work in progress inventories too high?
4. Transportation—Do you move materials efficiently?
5. Over-processing—Do you work on the product too many times, or otherwise work inefficiently?
6. Motion—Do people and equipment move between tasks efficiently?
7. Defects—How much time do you spend finding and fixing production mistakes?
8. Workforce—Do you use workers efficiently?

Lean Manufacturing is a technique that mainly focuses on eliminating waste in the production sector. It offers many tools, such as JIT, Kanban, Zero Defects, and 5S, among many others. While Lean Manufacturing has a lot of tools, it cannot compare with the extensive list of tools that Six Sigma offers. In fact, many experts combine both, which is known as Lean Sigma.

JIT is a great technique that assists manufacturing enterprises in improving efficiency in production and also has quality implications. It is usually implemented along with Kanban. Kanban is a key technique to involve people in the Lean process, from suppliers to customers. It helps eliminate the waste from inventory and overproduction. In addition, Zero Defects focuses on getting the product right the first time rather than spending extra time and money fixing poor quality products. The Zero Defects system reinforces the notion that no defect is acceptable, and encourages people to do things right the first time. The 5S philosophy relies on standardization and the 5S system focuses on sort, set in order, shine, standardize, and sustain. It is used to eliminate waste in work areas (MindTools 2016).

6.10 *Measuring efficiency*

Mohr et al. (2012) at McKinsey & Company stated that by taking a comprehensive approach to resource productivity, companies can improve Efficiency while strengthening their value propositions to customers and benefiting society as a whole. Their experiences suggest that manufacturers could reduce the amount of energy they use in production by 20%–30%. They could also design their products to reduce material use by 30% while increasing their potential for recycling and reuse. Indeed, companies could cut their product costs in half by reusing materials and components. Most Efficiency efforts focus on classic improvement approaches, such as Lean Manufacturing and 5S. Lean Manufacturing has had a tremendous impact not only in improving companies' Productivity, but also in improving companies' Efficiency. Since these techniques lack a systematic approach that focuses attention on resources throughout the value chain, manufacturers have tended to think narrowly about Efficiency (Mohr et al. 2012).

Energy and materials are frequently wasted in the manufacturing world. It requires a systematic approach to monitor Efficiency and make improvements. For example, Mohr et al. discuss the case of a car manufacturer that reduced by 15% the amount of energy consumed in assembly by simply optimizing ventilation processes. Innovation and R&D play an important role in Efficiency improvements that reduce production costs. Efficiency efforts can be carried along with sustainability initiatives, which have become very popular in the past couple of decades. Efficiency must be part of the organization's culture and be endorsed by suppliers and outsourced businesses. A key to meet delivery deadlines is to have on-time suppliers' delivery and other outsourced companies involved in the production process to deliver their materials and services on time. Although companies do not have exclusive control over these processes, they can influence suppliers and outsourcing companies by increasing the productivity and efficiency of their supply chains (Mohr et al. 2012).

Efficiency relies on time management and the ability of a company to optimize its resources and minimize its waste. Since manufacturing businesses have waste involved in their processes, an approach to measure efficiency holistically is needed. Equation 6.3 illustrates the MF for efficiency, which presents a new approach of measuring efficiency based on Resources, such as human capital, material, and energy and Waste, such as defects and downtime. An extended literature review was performed in order to develop the efficiency MF.

$$
\begin{aligned}
Efficiency\,(Plant,\,Year) = \;& Labor + Material + Energy \\
& + Production\,Capability + (1 - Defects) \\
& + Recycle + (1 - Downtime) + (1 - Inventories)
\end{aligned}
$$

$$(6.3)$$

where:

Efficiency (Plant, Year) = Efficiency MF
Labor = expected labor cost/actual labor cost
Material = expected material cost/actual material cost
Energy = expected energy cost/actual energy cost
Production Capability = maximum manpower × (production volume/ total no. of employees)
Defects = defect percentage
Recycle = recycle recovery/total waste

Downtime = percentage of downtime
Inventories = percentage of inventory turnover

6.11   Efficiency weight

The efficiency MF is illustrated in Figure 6.5, which is considered by all manufacturing experts, independently of their sector, one of the least important components of company success with a weight of 0.101, which represents 10.1% of the total weight of the company success model. The only component that has been assigned less weight than efficiency is employee morale with a weight of 0.098. The inconsistency ratio is 0.03, which is less than 0.1. This validates that the weight is appropriate and experts are consistent with their values.

The following table presents the efficiency taxonomy represented by two subcomponents, Resources and Waste. These two are key to efficiency, and a series of performance measures and metrics are identified under them. While there are many characterizations of efficiency, Table 6.15 summarizes the best performance measures found.

A metric has been identified per performance measure, and the following list provides a greater understanding of each efficiency metric.

- Labor—Expected labor cost/actual labor cost per unit
- Material—Expected material cost/actual material cost per unit
- Energy—Expected energy cost/actual energy cost per unit
- Production capability—Maximum manpower × (production volume/ employee)
- Defects—Defects cost or actual no. of defects or [1–(first pass yield)]
- Recycle—Recycle recovery (scrap + trimming)/total waste cost (scrap cost + waste disposal)
- Downtime—Downtime cost or percentage of downtime caused by machine, material, and planning
- Inventories—Percentage of inventory turnover on finished goods

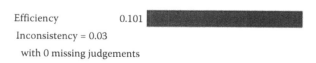

Efficiency   0.101

Inconsistency = 0.03

with 0 missing judgements

Figure 6.5 Efficiency weight.

Table 6.15 Efficiency performance measures

Component	Subcomponents	Performance measures	Metrics
Efficiency	Resources (direct cost)	Labor	Expected labor cost/actual labor cost
		Material	Expected material cost/ actual material cost
		Energy	Expected energy cost/ actual energy cost
		Production capability	Maximum manpower × (production volume/employee)
	Waste (direct cost)	Defects (mistakes, errors, etc.)	Defects cost
		Recycle/total waste	Recycle recovery/total cost
		Downtime	Percentage of downtime
		Inventories	Percentage of inventory turnover

6.12   Case example on efficiency

As mentioned before, Pam Rogers' subsidiaries are managed by type of goods. Plant A is a manufacturing plant that focuses on commercial products while Plant B is a manufacturing plant that focuses on residential products. When it comes to efficiency measures, Pam's company is decentralized and every subsidiary collects its respective data. Therefore, she does not have a holistic perspective of how her subsidiaries are doing when it comes to, for example waste and the utilization of resources.

Since there is no holistic efficiency scale or index for manufacturing businesses, a scale was developed by subject matter experts. Therefore, Table 6.16 presents the scale used to develop the efficiency MF.

Table 6.16 Efficiency industry scale

Industry scale	Efficiency percentage
Low	65–79
Medium	80–85
High	86–100

6.12.1 Efficiency membership function

A sigmoidal MF was selected to reflect the efficiency component, which is illustrated in Figure 6.6. The smaller the efficiency, the lower is the degree of membership that represents the fuzzy set. The degree of membership increases as efficiency increases.

The lower boundary of the Efficiency MF is 65% and the upper boundary of the efficiency MF is 100% as given in Table 6.17. The

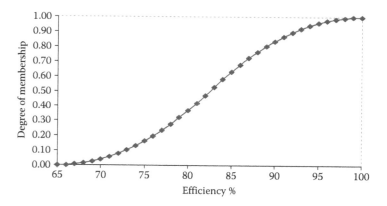

Figure 6.6 Efficiency MF.

Table 6.17 Efficiency MF values for the manufacturing industry

X—Efficiency %	Y—Degree of membership
65	0.00
70	0.04
75	0.16
80	0.37
81	0.42
82	0.47
83	0.53
84	0.58
85	0.63
90	0.84
95	0.96
100	1.00
Average—82.5	*0.5*
Min.—65	*0*
Max.—100	*1*

Table 6.18 Efficiency data from Plant A

Subcomp.	Factor variable	2002	2003	2004	2005
Resource (only direct cost)	Labor	0.99	0.95	0.93	0.89
	Material	1.03	1.00	1.03	0.91
	Energy	1.06	1.16	1.08	0.89
	Production capability	0.85	0.85	0.83	0.84
Waste (only direct cost)	Defects	$1-0.11 = 0.89$	$1-0.105 = 0.89$	$1-0.104 = 0.90$	$1-0.065 = 0.93$
	Recycle	0.937	1.04	1.641	1.47
	Downtime	$1-0.1 = 0.9$	$1-0.1 = 0.9$	$1-0.1 = 0.9$	$1-0.1 = 0.9$
	Inventories	$1-0.175 = 0.82$	$1-0.185 = 0.81$	$1-0.239 = 0.76$	$1-0.245 = 0.76$

previous graph shows that when the efficiency percentage is 65, the degree of membership is 0, so it barely belongs to the function; however, at 100%, efficiency fully belongs to the MF since the degree of membership is 1.

Table 6.18 presents the efficiency data collected from Plant A. Efficiency was measured by comparing the direct hours worked on each unit with the hours earned, excluding the indirect labor. Efficiency looks into the amount of resources used to produce each unit; the lower the amount of resources used and the higher amount of units produced, the better the efficiency level. All the metrics are expressed in ratios in order to be easily combined for model validation. Some factor variables, such as defects, downtime, and inventory, were subtracted from 1 in order to be appropriately included in the overall efficiency calculation. Inventory was measured by tracking cycle count adjustments, conducting annual full physical inventories, and through the tracking of inventory turns.

After calculating the efficiency percentage of Plant A from 2002 to 2005, Table 6.19 summarizes it. Overall, Plant A has done very well in efficiency.

Table 6.20 presents the efficiency percentage or X-values and the corresponding degree of membership or Y-values, as well as the total value obtained from multiplying the degree of membership by the weights. The total values were obtained by multiplying the degree of membership by the weight. The purpose of calculating the total values is to fit them within the company success model.

Table 6.19 Summarized efficiency data from Plant A

Year	2002	2003	2004	2005
Efficiency percentage	97	100	100	100

Table 6.20 Efficiency MF values for Plant A

Plant A	Efficiency percentage	Degree of membership	Total value
2002	97	0.99	0.0995
2003	100	1.00	0.1010
2004	100	1.00	0.1010
2005	100	1.00	0.1010

Table 6.21 Efficiency data from Plant B

Subcomp.	Factor variable	2003	2004	2005	2006
Resource (only direct cost)	Labor	0.81	0.72	0.79	0.91
	Material	0.82	0.69	0.68	0.94
	Energy	0.85	0.92	0.82	1.22
	Production capability	0.69	0.67	0.93	0.91
Waste (only direct cost)	Defects	$1-0.13 = 0.87$	$1-0.149 = 0.85$	$1-0.112 = 0.89$	$1-0.1323 = 0.87$
	Recycle	0.616	1.224	1.038	1.4507
	Downtime	$1-0.018 = 0.98$	$1-0.018 = 0.98$	$1-0.045 = 0.96$	$1-0.037 = 0.96$
	Inventories	$1-0.1028 = 0.9$	$1-0.1105 = 0.89$	$1-0.1307 = 0.87$	$1-0.1171=0.88$

Table 6.21 presents the data collected in Plant B. As observed, factor variables, such as defects, downtime, and inventories, were subtracted rom 1 in order to be appropriately included within the efficiency calculation.

Table 6.22 represents the overall percentage of efficiency obtained in Plant B. While this subsidiary was not as efficient as Plant A, over the years it improved. From 2002 to 2005, more data was collected yearly that was included in the MF. That is the challenge of finding historical data available in many organizations in order to make estimations and predict future performance.

Table 6.23 presents the percentage of efficiency or X-values, the degree of membership or Y-values, and the total values generated by multiplying the degree of membership by the weight.

Production reports, as well as accounting projections, among other documents, were used to identify historical data within this component. Plant A has had a historically better efficiency record than Plant B.

Table 6.22 Summarized efficiency data from Plant B

Year	2002	2003	2004	2005
Efficiency percentage	76	85	85	100

Table 6.23 Efficiency MF values for Plant B

Plant B	Efficiency percentage	Degree of membership	Total value
2003	76	0.20	0.0200
2004	85	0.63	0.0639
2005	85	0.63	0.0639
2006	100	1.00	0.1010

6.13   Summary

In conclusion, this chapter presents three new MFs developed for profit, productivity, and efficiency. Since these components have been widely characterized and measured, there is no need to develop a Fuzzy model per component in order to integrate them in the overall index. These MFs provide a simple mechanism to characterize and measure these components in manufacturing businesses. These functions can be used by any organizational leader or manufacturing manager to assess profit, productivity, and efficiency in their own enterprises and to also integrate them into a bigger model. That is the case with the company success index model.

References

Bureau of Labor Statistics. 2016. *Overview of BLS Productivity Statistics*. September 1, http://www.bls.gov/bls/productivity.htm

Inman, R. A. 2016. Revised by Gerhard Plenert. *Productivity Concepts and Measures*. Reference for Business. Copyright Advameg, Inc. Accessed November 12, 2016. http://www.referenceforbusiness.com/management/Pr-Sa/Productivity-Concepts-and-Measures.html

Investopedia. 2016. *Capacity Utilization Rate Definition*. Accessed November 14, 2016. http://www.investopedia.com/terms/c/capacityutilizationrate.asp#ixzz4Q2MyRAU0

Microbuspub. Classification of manufacturing costs and expenses, Chapter 4. Accessed November 5, 2016. http://www.microbuspub.com/pdfs/chapter4.pdf

MindTools. 2016. *Lean Manufacturing: Working More Efficiently*. Copyright Mind Tools Ltd. Accessed November 15, 2016. https://www.mindtools.com/pages/article/newSTR_44.htm

MIT Press. Information systems: Introduction and concepts, Chapter 1. Accessed November 7, 2016. https://mitpress.mit.edu/sites/default/files/titles/content/9780262015387_sch_0001.pdf

Mohr, S., Somers, K., Swartz, S., and H. Vanthournout. 2012. Manufacturing resources productivity. June, http://www.mckinsey.com/business-functions/sustainability-and-resource-productivity/our-insights/manufacturing-resource-productivity

National Association of Manufacturers. 2016. *Work Safety.* http://www.nam.org/
    Issues/Workplace-Safety/#sthash.os5knvGX.dpufhttp://www.nam.org/
    Issues/Workplace-Safety/
University of Missouri-St. Louis (UMSL). Information systems for business
    functions, Chapter 12. Accessed November 5, 2016. http://www.umsl.
    edu/~joshik/msis480/chapt12.htm
U.S. Census Bureau. 2016a. Net income after tax average of U.S. manufacturing
    corporations based on the quarterly financial report for manufacturing,
    mining, and trade corporations. U.S. Department of Commerce. https://
    www.census.gov/econ/qfr/
U.S. Census Bureau. 2016b. *Survey of Plant Capacity Utilization.* Department
    of Commerce. Accessed November 14, 2016. http://www.census.gov/
    manufacturing/capacity/
Wikipedia. 2016. https://en.wikipedia.org/wiki/Cost_accounting

chapter seven

A company success index model for manufacturing organizations

Pam Rogers, as previously discussed, is eager to have a company success index model that summarizes all the key components and performance measures in her business. While she has now a quality or employee morale model, she wants to know how she is doing overall in her sites or against competitors. Information that is used to measure, predict, and make better decisions is key and fundamental for managers to lead the market.

A company success index model that manufacturing leaders can easily implement to assess and predict organizational success in manufacturing organizations is presented in this chapter.

7.1 Company success index model development

Traditional modeling techniques tend to eliminate or explain uncertainty by excluding factor variables that cannot be explained, leading to inaccurate models caused by lost data. FST focuses on the possibility rather than a probability of predicting imprecise and uncontrollable data. Therefore, a company success index was developed, leading organizational managers and leaders toward a more clear understanding and evaluation of company success. To develop the organizational success index, FST was selected as the technique to identify the company success level. In addition, linguistic approaches were previously applied and developed for use in FST allowing factor variables to be used in terms that can be assigned a fuzzy numerical value. One of the most important advantages of using this technique is the opportunity to bring a scale for evaluating an environment conducive to company success.

Traditional uncertainty techniques ignore relevant independent variables from the model while MFs consider small impact variables within the model development process. The development of MFs is done through mapping functions, and these types of functions helped to develop predictive model factors such as ergonomics and safety, quality, employee morale, and company success. The goal of MFs is to map all the variables on an interval [0, 1], ensuring that important information about the response variable is kept and appropriately represented. MFs can be developed by performing a literature review or through the use of SMEs. Since linguistic variables differ among experts, MFs are developed through mapping functions. These are some of the benefits of using the MF approach and the FST technique:

- The combination of MFs assisted in the development of FST models which generated indexes capable of predicting organizational performance metrics essential to achieving company success.
- Easy assessment of company performance can be performed by using the described index models; any value less than 1.0 implies that a company is not achieving its best, and 0 represents a low organizational performance. Therefore, companies with an index well below 1.0 should investigate the reasons and improve their performance.
- FST index models allow organizational decision makers to measure and compare performance across multiple divisions. In addition, organizations can use these index models as a benchmarking tool to compare themselves with industry competitors.

A company success index model is presented in this final chapter where the MFs and models presented in the previous chapters are combined to provide a holistic perspective of the company with a simple percentage. The company success model represents a total of 64 quantitative and qualitative performance measures that any manufacturing leader in the United States could use to know where the company stands and what needs to be improved. Manufacturing leaders now have a new approach and model to evaluate and predict organizational success.

7.2   Weights

SMEs from industry and academia did a pairwise comparison in order to calculate the weights. Figure 7.1 illustrates the weights of company success obtained from the AHP performed by Expert Choice. These weights show the importance these areas have for manufacturing leaders. Profit represents more than twice the next weight, which is productivity. In fact, if the figure is turned 90°, it is easier to realize that the weights can be clustered in three groups: (1) profit, (2) productivity, ergonomics and safety, and quality, and (3) efficiency and employee morale. Financial excellence continues to be the most important component for manufacturing leaders. Second, productivity, quality, and employees' safety/ergonomics are also important for organizational decision makers. Third, it is not surprising

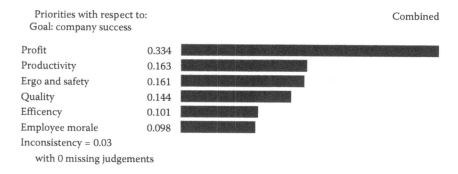

Figure 7.1 Company success index model weights.

to find employee morale to be the least important component for company leaders. While efficiency is not the least important component, its weight is almost as low as employee morale.

The following section focuses on the formulation of the Fuzzy models and MFs required to build the company success model. All the formulations presented in this book are reviewed in Section 7.3.

7.3 Company success index model formulation

All the factor variables identified in this book under profit, productivity, efficiency, ergonomics and safety, quality, and employee morale are now combined to calculate the company success index model. Equation 7.1 presents the company success index model that combines 64 quantitative and qualitative performance measures in a single equation. This model summarizes all the factors in a single figure from 0 to 1, which can be converted to a percentage of organizational success. This model assists manufacturing leaders to continuously improve organizational performance and achieve business excellence.

$$Company\ Success\ (Plant, Year) = (Wp \times Profit) + (Wpr \times Productivity)$$
$$+ (We \times Efficiency) + (Wq \times Quality)$$
$$+ (Wes \times Ergo.Safety)$$
$$+ (Wem \times Employee\ Morale) \qquad (7.1)$$

where (variables are represented by degree of membership):
  Company Success (Plant, Year) = company success index model
  Wp = weight of *Profit* component
  Profit = profit MF
  Wpr = weight of productivity component

Productivity = productivity MF
We = weight of efficiency component
Efficiency = efficiency MF
Wq = weight of quality component
Quality = quality index model
Wes = weight of ergonomics and safety component
Ergonomics and Safety = ergonomics and safety index model
Wem = weight of employee morale
Employee Morale = employee morale index model. The weights are
     obtained from applying AHP to SMEs' opinions

MFs and models were combined using additive modeling and were validated by calculating the accuracy against gold standards. The total values were calculated by multiplying weights by degree of membership. It is by building MFs that all the performance measures with different units become a value from 0 to 1.

7.4   Company success index model validation

Previously developed organizational performance measure models, tools, and approaches considered company success to be highly dependable and solely represented by the organization's strategy. The reality is that no matter how much variation exists between different organizations, the main goal of any company leader is to own the market or become the market leader. Table 7.1 represents the overall company success MFs, such as profit, productivity, and efficiency, as well as the model value, such as ergonomics and safety, employee morale, and quality. The table compares the company success index model figures with the gold standard or market share (based on *Profit*) position of the organization (under study, Plant A and Plant B) in the U.S. market. The gold standard selected to evaluate company success was market share, which is the primary goal of any

Table 7.1 Company success values versus gold standard for Plant A and Plant B

Data source	Year	Profit	Productivity	Efficiency	Quality	Ergo. and safety	Employee morale	Total	Gold standard
Plant A	2002	0.1397	0.1630	0.0929	0.0737	0.1201	0.0461	0.6355	0.30
Plant A	2003	0.1637	0.1630	0.0969	0.0736	0.1231	0.0461	0.6663	0.30
Plant A	2004	0.1666	0.1630	0.0969	0.0740	0.1252	0.0461	0.6716	0.30
Plant A	2005	0.2265	0.1630	0.1010	0.0730	0.1251	0.0461	0.7348	0.30
Plant B	2003	0.0081	0.1630	0.0477	0.0735	0.1133	0.0559	0.4614	0.17
Plant B	2004	0.0109	0.1630	0.0731	0.0717	0.1125	0.0559	0.4870	0.17
Plant B	2005	0.0165	0.1630	0.0731	0.0778	0.0827	0.0559	0.4690	0.17
Plant B	2006	0.0173	0.1630	0.1003	0.0741	0.1375	0.0559	0.5481	0.16

organization (JP Morgan 2006). Since employee morale was only measured in Plant A in 2005 and in Plant B in 2006, the same values were used as historical data to have a completed model. As Pam continues measuring this component, the model will be more accurate in future applications.

From Table 7.1, it can be observed how company success for Plant A is higher than that for Plant B. This makes sense since the majority of the company success components are higher in Plant A than in Plant B. This trend is captured across this book. Market share or company success gold standard follows the following scale: low 0%–10%, medium 11%–20%, and high 21%–100%. Table 7.2 represents the scale developed to interpret the company success figures.

Table 7.3 compares the company success linguistic results with the gold standard linguistic values. The majority of the results match, with the exception of Plant A in the year 2012.

Table 7.4 shows the accuracy calculations performed over the company success model.

This book has presented a company success index model for manufacturing enterprises that utilizes organizational performance measures. Organizational performance measures such as profit, productivity, efficiency, quality, employee morale, and ergonomics and safety were combined to generate an overall organizational model, which will enhance the decision-making process for leaders within manufacturing industries.

Table 7.2 FST for company success

FST level	Degree of membership
Low	0–0.33
Medium	0.34–0.66
High	0.67–1

Table 7.3 Company success Model versus gold standard fuzzy values for Plant A and Plant B

Location	Year	Company success model	Gold standard (market share)
Plant A	2012	Medium	High
Plant A	2013	High	High
Plant A	2014	High	High
Plant A	2015	High	High
Plant B	2013	Medium	Medium
Plant B	2014	Medium	Medium
Plant B	2015	Medium	Medium
Plant B	2016	Medium	Medium

Company success in manufacturing organizations

Table 7.4 Accuracy values of company success index model

Gold standard (market share)				
Company success model		True	False	
	Positive	TP = 7	FP = 0	$7/(7+0) = 100\%$
	Negative	FN = 1	TN = 0	0/1
				Accuracy
				$7/8 = 87.5\%$

The proposed methodology or approach presented in Chapter 2 provides an organizational measurement system ready to be benchmarked by any manufacturing organization (independently of unions). In addition, this book has presented a reliable model for quantifying quality, employee morale, ergonomics and safety, and company success which enhances the prediction and control of these critical areas within an organization. Furthermore, this manuscript illustrates a series of reliable tools, methods, and techniques that can be readily used by organizational leaders and operational managers to augment their decision-making in a highly dynamic environment. In addition, nonlinear models have been created to appropriately characterize constantly changing organizational environments consisting of large amounts of qualitative and quantitative data. Thus, the organizational success index model and methodology developed in this research provides organizational managers with a systematic approach to analyze complex decisions impacting company performance and business strategy. Furthermore, all the developed models may be used as a comparison tool for any manufacturing facility interested in evaluating their organizational performance against the industry average among various manufacturing enterprises. The company success index model was developed using three MFs describing profit, productivity, and efficiency in Chapter 6 as well as three Fuzzy index models characterizing employee morale in Chapter 3, quality in Chapter 4, and ergonomics and safety in Chapter 5.

The MFs provided an exceptional mapping approach to fit industry average data without losing important information that traditional modeling techniques would have eliminated or not taken into account. Components such as profit, productivity, and efficiency have been modeled in previous research; therefore, it was not necessary to develop Fuzzy models for the purpose of this research. However, it was necessary to develop MFs to appropriately combine these components with factors of quality, employee morale, and ergonomics and safety. Using MFs to successfully combine all the company success components was necessary to ensure that the corresponding degree of membership was identified for each component within the Fuzzy model: degree of membership (0–1 range). Furthermore, additive modeling was applied to combine the individual component models to determine an aggregate value for company success. The relative weights of each individual component obtained from applying AHP to SME opinions were multiplied by degree of membership obtained from the MFs and developed models.

The company success index model results were compared to the gold standard currently used by industries, which in this case is the market share position of the organization within the U.S. market. The market share from JP Morgan reports was selected as the gold standard to evaluate company success since this is the primary goal of any organization. Previously developed organizational performance measure models, tools, and approaches considered company success to be highly dependable and solely represented by the organization's strategy. The reality is that no matter how much variation exists between different organizations, the main goal of any company is to become the market leader. The resulting research model was validated considering information on market share. The company success index presented in this chapter is 87% accurate in determining company success in the manufacturing plants analyzed in this study.

Also, an employee morale index model was presented in Chapter 3 and an employee morale survey created. The index model includes an organizational decision aspect, the WTP prioritization technique ready to be used by HR managers or corporate leaders to make wiser investment decisions on human capital. After performing an extensive literature review on employee morale, the 100 Best Companies to Work For index was used as a gold standard for model comparison. Therefore, a comparison between the Ferreras model and the 100 Best Companies to Work for index model was performed. This model is validated and the accuracy of the model is 100%. This book has presented a valid overall company success index as well as individual models describing the level of employee morale, quality, ergonomics and safety that can be implemented to augment the decision-making process in manufacturing organizations.

Furthermore, after performing an extended literature review on quality, the CoQ model was identified as the most appropriate approach to validate the quality index model presented in Chapter 4. The CoQ model consists of four cost factor variables: prevention, appraisal, internal failure, and external failure. A holistic approach was created to characterize organizational quality in this research by adding new factor variables that bring the customer's perspective, such as customer satisfaction and customer loyalty. A successful quality index model was presented in Chapter 4, which was validated with 87% accuracy in representing the level of quality in a manufacturing organization.

After performing an extended literature review in ergonomics and safety, no deterministic model was found to exist that evaluated and combined factor variables such as annual replacement cost (extra wages generated by an injury, illness, or accident), lost workday cases, OSHA fines, OSHA recordable cases, workers' compensation expenses, and pro-active ergonomic activities to present an overall aggregate describing ergonomics and safety; therefore, an ergonomics and safety model was developed and presented in Chapter 5. Additive mathematical operands were applied to combine all the ergonomics and safety MFs and develop the mathematical model. The ergonomics and safety model was validated and the resulting model is 87% accurate in representing the ergonomics and safety level of manufacturing organizations.

7.5   Case example

The methodology and approach developed in this research can be applied to any manufacturing enterprise, independent of the type of product manufactured. To illustrate how this methodology and approach can be applied, a case example is presented based on the Boeing Company. If Boeing wanted to implement the research methodology illustrated in this manuscript, Boeing would have to complete steps in Sections 7.5.1 through 7.5.6.

7.5.1   Step 1: Taxonomies development/key organizational performance measures

The first step is to develop taxonomies for all the company success com-ponents (profit, productivity, efficiency, quality, employee morale, and ergonomics and safety) to be evaluated. The taxonomies characterize components, subcomponents, and factor variables affecting organiza-tional success in the aerospace manufacturing industry. In addition, key organizational performance measures or metrics should be identified using various techniques, such as a literature review and SMEs.

7.5.2   Step 2: Identify data collection tools, methods, and techniques

Existing tools, methods, and techniques currently in place at the Boeing company should be evaluated to identify historical data that can be obtained. The organizational leader questionnaire should be adminis-tered to Boeing executives to facilitate the organizational performance measures data collection process. The organizational leader question-naire is distributed and used initially to identify the organizational deci-sion-making challenges that the manufacturing leaders are dealing with and the type of tool that will help them achieve organizational success (see Appendix A).

Furthermore, the plant manager questionnaire developed should be sent along with the list of performance measures, metrics, and definitions to the plant manager or operations manager (see Appendix B). This step is critically important since it helps identify the key performance measures and metrics currently measured and the tools used in the business to collect the historical data. This step also provides a better understanding of the amount of data collection and estimation that will be required to evaluate the organizational success of the enterprise. A glossary of terms is developed and provided to avoid any misunderstanding of the key performance measures and metrics identified, as well as to enhance the success and accuracy of the data collection process (see Appendix C).

7.5.3   Step 3: Data collection

This step is very important in the process since it should involve the collection of all the data, the historic data and the collection of measures that have never been collected before. Approximations using existing data should be first pursued, followed by data collection of those measures that cannot be estimated otherwise.

7.5.4   Step 4: Model development per company success component using the fuzzy set theory

The following concepts and techniques must be considered in this step:

* Literature review must be performed in order to find industry data from the specific industry. The more historical data found with good data integrity, the more accurate the index model will be. Otherwise, SMEs will have to provide data based on their expert opinions.
* The development of MFs is a key part of developing Fuzzy models. The MFs should be developed based on the data obtained from the literature review or SMEs. National averages, indexes, and scales are ideal to develop good MFs.
* Use the AHP to identify the weights for the various factor variables within the index models; SMEs will do a pairwise comparison exercise in order to run the AHP analysis. The weights can be obtained after inputting the SMEs' feedback into Expert Choice, one of the AHP software programs available. The inconsistency ratio must be observed to assure that the SMEs' judgments are consistent. The following equations—Equation 7.2 for profit, Equation 7.3 for productivity, and Equation 7.4 for efficiency—are three major components of company success that are represented by the following MFs.

$$Profit \ (Plant, Year) = Revenue - Expenses \qquad (7.2)$$

where:

Profit (Plant, Year) = profit MF

Revenue = sales (annually)

Expenses = factor variables, such as labor, material, variable over-head, fixed overhead, variable cost, income tax, legal fees, R&D expenses, among others. The following equation represents productivity

$$Production\ (Plant, Year) = \frac{Production\ Volume}{(Production\ Volume + Backlog)} \qquad (7.3)$$

where:

Production (Plant, Year) = production MF (capacity utilization)

Production Volume = amount of units produced

Backlog = amount of units never built.

The following MF represents efficiency.

$$Efficiency\ (Plant, Year) = Labor + Material + Energy$$
$$+ Production\ Capability + (1 - Defects) \qquad (7.4)$$
$$+ Recycle + (1 - Downtime) + (1 - Inventories)$$

where:

Efficiency (Plant, Year) = efficiency MF

Labor = expected labor cost/actual labor cost

Material = expected material cost/actual material cost

Energy = expected energy cost/actual energy cost

Production Capability = maximum manpower × (production volume/ total number of employees)

Defects = defect percentage

Recycle = recycle recovery/total waste

Downtime = percentage of downtime

Inventories = percentage of inventory turnover

The following equations—Equation 7.5 for ergonomics and safety, Equation 7.6 for quality, and Equation 7.7 for employee morale—are three major components of company success that are represented by the following new Fuzzy models. The following model represents ergonomics and safety.

$$ES\ (Plant, Year) = (W_{WW} \times WW) + (W_{LWDC} \times LWDC) + (W_{OSHA} \times OSHA)$$
$$+ (W_{II} \times II) + (W_{PE} \times PE) + (W_{WC} \times WC) \qquad (7.5)$$

where:
  ES = ergonomics and safety index value
  W_{WW} = replacement cost weight
  WW = replacement cost degree of membership
  W_{LWDC} = lost workday cases weight
  $LWDC$ = lost workday cases degree of membership
  W_{OSHA} = OSHA fines weight
  $OSHA$ = OSHA fines degree of membership
  W_{II} = OSHA injury and illness weight
  II = OSHA injury and illness degree of membership
  W_{PE} = proactive ergonomics weight
  PE = proactive ergonomics degree of membership
  W_{WC} = workers' compensation weight
  WC = workers' compensation degree of membership

The following model represents quality.

$$Q\,(Plant, Year) = (W_{PC} \times PC) + (W_{AC} \times AC) + (W_{IC} \times IC)$$
$$+ (W_{EC} \times EC) + (W_{CS} \times CS) + (W_{CL} \times CL) \qquad (7.6)$$

where:
  Q = quality index value
  W_{PC} = prevention cost weight
  PC = prevention cost degree of membership
  W_{AC} = appraisal cost weight
  AC = appraisal cost degree of membership
  W_{IC} = internal failure cost weight
  IC = internal failure cost degree of membership
  W_{EC} = external failure cost weight
  EC = external failure cost degree of membership
  W_{CS} = customer satisfaction cost weight
  CS = customer satisfaction cost degree of membership
  W_{CL} = customer loyalty cost weight
  CL = customer loyalty cost degree of membership

The following model represents the employee morale model.

$$EM\,(Plant, Year) = WE + EE \qquad (7.7)$$

where:
  EM *(Plant, Year)* represents the employee morale component
  WE represents the Work Environment subcomponent
  EE represents the Employee Engagement subcomponent

To obtain the identified employee morale subcomponents, the following mathematical equations were used: Equation 7.8 representing Work Environment and Equation 7.9 representing Employee Engagement.

$$WE\,(Plant,Year) = (W_1 \times X_1) + (W_2 \times X_2) + (W_3 \times X_3) + (W_4 \times X_4)$$
$$+ (W_5 \times X_5) + (W_6 \times X_6) + (W_7 \times X_7)$$
$$+ (W_8 \times X_8) + (W_9 \times X_9) + (W_{10} \times X_{10}) \tag{7.8}$$

where (all units are included within the indicators/metrics table):
   WE represents the *Work Environment* subcomponent
   W_1 represents the weight of open communication
   X_1 is the level of open line of communication with management
   W_2 represents the weight of recognition and rewards
   X_2 is the level of recognition and rewards by management
   W_3 represents the weight of advancement opportunities
   X_3 is the level of advancement opportunities
   W_4 represents the weight of teamwork
   X_4 is the level of teamwork
   W_5 represents the weight of compensation
   X_5 is the level of compensation
   W_6 represents the weight of training
   X_6 is the level of training opportunities
   W_7 represents the weight of supervisory consultation
   X_7 is the level of comfortable supervisory consultation
   W_8 represents the weight of company policies and guidelines
   X_8 is the level of fair company policies and guidelines
   W_9 represents the weight of company values
   X_9 is the level of company values within an organization
   W_{10} represents the weight of work flexibility
   X_{10} is the level of work flexibility

$$EE\,(Plant,\,Year) = (W_{11} \times X_{11}) + (W_{12} \times X_{12}) + (W_{13} \times X_{13}) + (W_{14} \times X_{14})$$
$$+ (W_{15} \times X_{15}) + (W_{16} \times X_{16}) + (W_{17} \times X_{17}) + (W_{18} \times X_{18})$$
$$+ (W_{19} \times X_{19}) + (W_{20} \times X_{20}) + (W_{21} \times X_{21}) \tag{7.9}$$

where:
   EE represents the *Employee Engagement* subcomponent
   W_{11} represents the weight of belonging
   X_{11} is the level of belonging to a work team/work family
   W_{12} represents the weight of involving
   X_{12} the level of involvement in decision-making and company activities

W_{13} represents the weight of enthusiasm
X_{13} the level of enthusiasm about your Job
W_{14} represents the weight of motivation
X_{14} is the level of motivation
W_{15} represents the weight of commitment
X_{15} is the level of commitment and devotion to work
W_{16} represents the weight of loyalty
X_{16} is the level of loyalty to the organization
W_{17} represents the weight of trust
X_{17} is the level of trust in management
W_{18} represents the weight of appreciation
X_{18} is the level of appreciation by supervisor
W_{19} represents the weight of empowerment
X_{19} is the level of empowerment to make own decisions
W_{20} represents the weight of absenteeism
X_{20} is the percentage of absenteeism
W_{21} represents the weight of turnover
X_{21} is the percentage of turnover

7.5.5   Step 5: Company success index model

Combining all the critical success factor variables that affect the overall company success (profit, productivity, efficiency, ergonomics and safety, quality, and employee morale) was essential to generate an index capable of measuring the relative performance of company success. The following *Company Success* index model, Equation 7.10, could be benchmarked by other manufacturing organizations, and assist others to continuously improve organizational performance and achieve manufacturing excellence.

$$
\begin{aligned}
\textit{Company Success (Plant, Year)} = {} & (Wp \times Profit) + (Wpr \times Productivity) \\
& + (We \times Efficiency) + (Wq \times Quality) \\
& + (Wes \times Ergo\ Safety) \\
& + (Wem \times Employee\ Morale)
\end{aligned}
\tag{7.10}
$$

where:
  Company Success (Plant, Year) = company success index model
  Wp = weight of profit
  Profit = profit MF
  Wpr = weight of productivity
  Productivity = productivity MF
  We = weight of efficiency

Efficiency = efficiency MF
Wq = weight of quality
Quality = quality index model
Wes = weight of ergonomics and safety
Ergonomics and Safety = ergonomics and safety index model
Wem = weight of employee morale
Employee Morale = employee morale index model.

7.5.6 Step 6: Company success index model validation

Profit, earnings, gain, income, and market position are commonly known as measures of success in an enterprise. However, the ultimate goal of any organizational leader is to own the market. Therefore, market share is used as the gold standard of company success. Accuracy calculations must be performed to validate all the models. Gold standards must be identified and linguistic scales must be developed to appropriately validate all the index models.

7.6 Summary

This book provides a holistic characterization of company success based quantitative and qualitative performance measures that represent profit, productivity, efficiency, quality, ergonomics and safety, and employee morale. The unique methodology and approach described in this book integrates a variety of tools, methods, and techniques to develop a mathematical index model capable of combining 64 factor variables. The combined effect of these components and their performance measures is achieved through a series of reliable models and MFs that assist organizational managers and leaders in making wiser decisions in key areas. Furthermore, a company success index model has been presented to assess and predict organizational performance in manufacturing organizations. Lastly, this book has presented a series of tools, methods, and techniques useful in measuring and assessing organizational performance in manufacturing organizations. This chapter has described a reliable company success index model ready to be used by enterprise leaders and benchmarked by other sectors.

Reference

Morgan, J. P. 2006. *HVAC Industry*. 2005–2006 Industry Review & Outlook.

Appendix A: Organizational leader questionnaire

Instructions: An organizational leader should fill out this questionnaire. Please include the job description along with your answers.

1. What type of organizational decisions do you most frequently encounter?
2. How are your decisions the majority of the times? Please assign a percentage to the following categories: (simple vs. complex, expected vs. unexpected, etc.)
   a. Simple _____%
   b. Complex _____%
   c. Expected _____%
   d. Unexpected _____%
   e. Have enough information _____%
   f. Do not have enough information _____%
   g. Others:_____
3. What are the external and uncontrollable forces that affect organizational decisions?
4. Would you use something else besides your experience to make organizational decisions? Y/N
5. What type of organizational decisions would you like help with?
   a. Daily decisions
   b. Monthly decisions
   c. Annual decisions
   d. Others:_____
6. What organizational decisions are the most challenging?
   a. The ones related to employees
   b. The ones that must be made without having all the information
   c. The ones that must be made having too much information
   d. Others:_____

7. What type of information would you need to make more appropriate organizational decisions?
8. What is the importance that each component has in making organizational decisions? Please prioritize them (considering 1—*most important* and 6—*least important*).
   a. Profit
   b. Productivity
   c. Efficiency
   d. Quality
   e. Safety and Ergonomics
   f. Employee Morale
9. Do you determine the importance of each component or are they determined by your immediate supervisor?
10. What is the most stressful factor when you have to make an organizational decision?

Comments and Suggestions: (if you consider there is any additional information which would help me design a decision tool that fits your necessities, please express your comments/suggestions in this section). Thank you for your valuable time and consideration!

Appendix B: Plant manager questionnaire

Instructions: The plant manager or operations manager should fill out this questionnaire with the assistance of managers in charge of the following areas: profit (accounting manager), productivity (production manager), efficiency (demand forecasting manager), quality (quality manager), ergonomics and safety (safety and ergonomics managers), and employee morale (human resources manager).

1. Have the following components been measured at your plant? (Y/N)
   a. Profit
   b. Productivity
   c. Efficiency
   d. Employee morale
   e. Safety
   f. Ergonomics
   g. Quality
2. Have the following subcomponents been measured at your plant? (Y/N)
   a. Revenue
   b. Expenses
   c. Output (production performance)
   d. Input (suppliers' performance)
   e. Resource (resource efficiency)
   f. Waste (waste efficiency)
   g. Work environment
   h. Employee's engagement
   i. Customer satisfaction
   j. Quality management and control
   k. Ergonomics and safety management and control

3. How do you evaluate employee's safety and ergonomics? Do you use any key performance measures identified in this model, such as OSHA recordable, etc.?
4. How do you evaluate quality within your organization? Do you use any key performance measures identified within this model, such as rework percentage, etc.?
5. How do you evaluate the plant's efficiency? Do you use any key performance measures identified in this work, such as production capability, etc.?
6. How do you evaluate the plant's productivity? Do you use any key performance measures identified in this characterization, such as production volume, etc.?
7. How do you evaluate employee morale within your plant? Do you use any key performance measures identified within this model, such absenteeism rate, employee's motivation, etc?
8. Do you offer professional development training and learning opportunities to your workers?
9. What type of audits do you perform (ISO 9001, OSHA audits, etc.)?
10. Do you have a union in your plant? If Yes, please explain how it is working.
11. Do you have continuous improvement activities in your plant (Six Sigma, Lean activities, etc.)? Please explain.
12. Do you perform customer satisfaction surveys and customer loyalty studies?
13. Have you ever measured the employee morale level within your plant? If so, how?

Appendix C: Glossary of terms

C.1 Quality terms

- Customer loyalty—Percentage of repeat customers based on annual amount spent.
- Customer satisfaction—Percentage of customers satisfied with products.
- Prevention costs
  - *Quality planning costs* include salaries of individuals associated with quality planning and problem-solving teams, as well as the development of new procedures, new equipment design, and reliability studies.
  - *Process control costs* include costs spent on analyzing production processes and implementing process control plans.
  - *Information systems costs* include expenses to develop data requirements and measurements.
  - *Training and general management costs* include internal and external training programs, clerical staff expenses (secretarial or assistant), and miscellaneous supplies.
- Appraisal costs
  - *Test and inspection costs* are costs associated with incoming materials, work-in-process, and finished goods (including equipment costs and salaries).
  - *Instrument maintenance costs* arise from calibration and repair of measuring instruments.
  - *Process measurement and control costs* involve the time spent by workers to gather and analyze quality measurements.
- Internal failure costs
  - *Scrap and rework costs* include material, labor, and overhead.
  - *Costs of corrective action* arise from time spent in determining the causes of failure and correcting production problems.
  - *Downgrading costs* include revenue lost when selling a product at a lower price when it does not meet specifications.

- *Process failure costs* include unplanned machine downtime or unplanned equipment repair.
- External failure costs
  - *Costs due to customer complaints and returns* include rework on returned items, cancelled orders, and freight premiums.
  - *Product recall costs and warranty claims* include the cost of repair or replacement as well as associated administrative costs.
  - *Product liability costs* result from legal actions and settlements.

(Cost of Quality definitions obtained from Evans and Lindsay [2002]).

C.2   Profit terms

- Sales—Net sales (production revenue).
- Labor—Wages of direct labor.
- Material—Material cost of raw material, excluding parts, containers, and supplies.
- Variable overhead—Variable expenses of a business which cannot be attributed to any specific business activity, but are still necessary for the business to function. For example, temporary workers' wages are included within this category.
- Fixed overhead cost—Fixed expenses of an organization that cannot be attributed to any specific business activity but are necessary for the business to function. For example, executive salaries are included within this category.
- Variable cost—A cost which varies as the production level varies. Producing more adds to variable cost, and producing less reduces variable cost.
- Income taxes—State and federal income tax generated by sales.
- Legal fees—Expenses allocated to legal activities or corporate premium for legal coverage.
- Research and development expenditures—Cost due to research and development efforts, such as customize products, new products, and value engineering.

C.3   Productivity terms

- Production volume—Total amount of units built per year.
- Delivery—Percentage of on-time units delivered to customer.
- Backlog—Amount of orders not met.
- Suppliers—Percentage of on-time material arrival from suppliers.

C.4 Efficiency terms

- Labor—Expected labor cost/actual labor cost per unit.
- Material—Expected material cost/actual material cost per unit.
- Energy—Expected energy cost/actual energy cost per unit.
- Production capability—Maximum manpower × (production volume/employee).
- Defects—Defects cost or actual no. of defects or [1−(first pass yield)].
- Recycle—Recycle recovery (scrap + trimming)/total waste cost (scrap cost + waste disposal).
- Downtime—Downtime cost or percentage of downtime caused by machine, material, and planning.
- Inventories—Percentage of inventory turnover on finished goods.

C.5 Ergonomics and Safety terms

- Replacement cost—Employee replacement cost after an injury has occurred.
- Lost work-day cases—Frequency rates of lost workday cases.
- OSHA—OSHA fines.
- OSHA recordable—Frequency rates of OSHA injuries or illnesses.
- Proactive ergonomics—Cost of proactive ergonomics, such as awareness training, ergonomics assessments, or cost to maintain an ergonomics program.
- Worker's compensation—Workers' compensation expenses, such as insurance premiums.

C.6 Employee Morale terms

- Absenteeism—Absenteeism rate.
- Turnover—Turnover rate.

Reference

Evans, J. R. and Lindsay, W. M. 2002. *The Management and Control of Quality*. Fifth Edition. Cincinnati, OH: South-Western Thompson Learning, pp. 115–462.

Appendix D: Employee morale survey

Department: _____ Sex: M/F Age: _____ Seniority: _____

This Employee Morale assessment tool has been designed to reveal what is your Employee Morale level based on a couple of areas: "Work Environment" and "Employee Engagement." Please mark your response to each of the questions below using the following scale:

Always = 4 points
Usually = 3 points
Sometimes = 2 points
Rarely = 1 point

D.1 Belonging

_____1. I feel a part of "the (Company Name) family."
_____2. I am treated more as a partner/team member than as an employee.

Is "feeling as if you belong to a work team/work family" an important factor for you to achieve high Employee Morale? **Yes** or **No** (circle correct answer).

How much would you be willing to sacrifice out of your paycheck per year to have the "feeling of belonging to a work team/work family"?

0	1	5	20	50
No	Very little	Moderate amount of	High amount of	A lot of

D.2   Open communication

_____3. Information is openly shared between management and employees.

_____4. Management gives all of the information I need to perform my job tasks.

Is "having an open line of communication with management" an important factor for you to achieve high Employee Morale? **Yes** or **No** (circle correct answer).

How much would you be willing to sacrifice out of your paycheck per year to have "an open line of communication with management"?

0	1	5	20	50
No	Very little	Moderate amount of	High amount of	A lot of

D.3   Recognition and rewards

_____5. At (Company Name), we are rewarded for our performance and for striving to achieve excellence.

_____6. My supervisor recognizes the extra effort and actions I do to perform the best job at (Company Name).

Is "being recognized and rewarded by management" an important factor for you to achieve high Employee Morale? **Yes** or **No** (circle correct answer).

How much would you be willing to sacrifice out of your paycheck per year to be "recognized and rewarded by management"?

0	1	5	20	50
No	Very little	Moderate amount of	High amount of	A lot of

D.4   Involving

_____7. My opinion is listened to by management when making decisions involving my work tasks.

_____8. I am involved in (Company Name) extracurricular activities such as sporting teams, etc.

Is "being involved in decision-making" an important factor for you to achieve high Employee Morale? **Yes** or **No** (circle correct answer).

How much are you willing to sacrifice out of your paycheck per year to "become more involved in decision-making and company activities"?

0	1	5	20	50
No	Very little	Moderate amount of	High amount of	A lot of

D.5   Enthusiasm

_____9. I find my work interesting and fulfilling.

_____10. I feel like a contributor to (Company Name) success.

Is "being enthusiastic about your job" an important factor for you to achieve high Employee Morale? **Yes** or **No** (circle correct answer).

How much are you willing to sacrifice out of your paycheck per year to "become more enthusiastic about your job"?

0	1	5	20	50
No	Very little	Moderate amount of	High amount of	A lot of

D.6   Advancement opportunities

_____11. (Company Name) provides plenty of opportunities for personal growth.

_____12. (Company Name) provides technical training so that I can advance in my career.

Is "being provided with advancement opportunities" an important factor for you to achieve high Employee Morale? **Yes** or **No** (circle correct answer).

How much would you be willing to sacrifice out of your paycheck per year to be "provided with more advancement opportunities"?

0	1	5	20	50
No	Very little	Moderate amount of	High amount of	A lot of

D.7   Motivation

_____13. At my department, the motivation level is *moderate to high* on a daily basis.

_____14. My work gives me a feeling of personal accomplishment.

Is "feeling motivated" an important factor for you to achieve high Employee Morale? **Yes** or **No** (circle correct answer).

How much would you be willing to sacrifice out of your paycheck per year to feel "more motivated"?

0	1	5	20	50
No	Very little	Moderate amount of	High amount of	A lot of

D.8   Commitment

_____15. I am dedicated to improving my performance every day.
_____16. I am devoted to the work tasks assigned.

Is "being committed to work" an important factor for you to achieve high Employee Morale? **Yes** or **No** (circle correct answer).

How much would you be willing to sacrifice out of your paycheck per year to feel "more committed and devoted to work"?

0	1	5	20	50
No	Very little	Moderate amount of	High amount of	A lot of

D.9   Loyalty

_____17. I am proud of being a (Company Name) employee.
_____18. I would like to grow and achieve my career goals within (Company Name).

Is "being loyal to (Company Name)" an important factor for you to achieve high Employee Morale? **Yes** or **No** (circle correct answer).

How much would you be willing to sacrifice out of your paycheck per year to become "more loyal to (Company Name)"?

0	1	5	20	50
No	Very little	Moderate amount of	High amount of	A lot of

D.10   Trust

_____19. I believe (Company Name) has a high level of ethics.
_____20. I trust top management's integrity.

Is "being able to trust management" an important factor for you to achieve high Employee Morale? **Yes** or **No** (circle correct answer).

How much would you be willing to sacrifice out of your paycheck per year to have "more trust in management"?

0	1	5	20	50
No	Very little	Moderate amount of	High amount of	A lot of

D.11 Appreciation

_____21. My supervisor always listens to my suggestions.

_____22. My supervisor always shows appreciation for every extra effort I put into my work.

Is "being appreciated by your supervisor" an important factor for you to achieve high Employee Morale? **Yes** or **No** (circle correct answer).

How much would you be willing to sacrifice out of your paycheck per year to be "more appreciated by your supervisor"?

0	1	5	20	50
No	Very little	Moderate amount of	High amount of	A lot of

D.12 Empowerment

_____23. My manager gives me enough opportunities to take an active role as a leader.

_____24. My job gives me enough opportunities and independence to use my skills and abilities to make my own decisions.

Is "being empowered to make your own decisions" an important factor for you to achieve high Employee Morale? **Yes** or **No** (circle correct answer).

How much would you be willing to sacrifice out of your paycheck per year to be "more empowered to make your own decisions"?

0	1	5	20	50
No	Very little	Moderate amount of	High amount of	A lot of

D.13 Teamwork

_____25. People within my group or department cooperate with each other rather than compete.

_____26. My supervisor encourages teamwork and cooperation to achieve targeted goals.

Is "working in teams" an important factor for you to achieve high Employee Morale? Yes or No (circle correct answer).

How much would you be willing to sacrifice out of your paycheck per year to have more "teamwork"?

0	1	5	20	50
No	Very little	Moderate amount of	High amount of	A lot of

D.14 Compensation

_____27. I am satisfied with my wages.
_____28. I would prefer working based on performance rather than for hourly rates or salary.

Is "being compensated" an important factor for you to achieve high Employee Morale? **Yes** or **No** (circle correct answer).

How much would you be willing to sacrifice out of your paycheck per year to have "more compensation"?

0	1	5	20	50
No	Very little	Moderate amount of	High amount of	A lot of

D.15 Training

_____29. My employer provides plenty resources and training opportunities.
_____30. (Company Name) facilitates ongoing training to upgrade my skills.

Is "being provided with training opportunities" an important factor for you to achieve high Employee Morale? **Yes** or **No** (circle correct answer).

How much would you be willing to sacrifice out of your paycheck per year to be "provided with more training opportunities"?

0	1	5	20	50
No	Very little	Moderate amount of	High amount of	A lot of

D.16 Supervisor consultation

_____31. I feel comfortable talking to my supervisor whenever there is a problem.
_____32. I like knowing my supervisor's point of view whenever I have to make an important decision.

Is "feeling comfortable consulting your supervisor" an important factor for you to achieve high Employee Morale? **Yes** or **No** (circle correct answer).

How much would you be willing to sacrifice out of your paycheck per year to feel "more comfortable consulting your supervisor"?

0	1	5	20	50
No	Very little	Moderate amount of	High amount of	A lot of

D.17 Company policies and guidelines

_____33. Policies and procedures are explained adequately within (Company Name).

_____34. Work policies are fair in this plant.

Are "fair company policies and guidelines" an important factor for you to achieve high Employee Morale? **Yes** or **No** (circle correct answer).

How much would you be willing to sacrifice out of your paycheck per year to have "fair company policies and guidelines"?

0	1	5	20	50
No	Very little	Moderate amount of	High amount of	A lot of

D.18 Company values

_____35. My personal values are similar to (Company Name) values.

_____36. Organizational values such as honesty, integrity, and ethics are observed at (Company Name).

Are "company values such as ethics and integrity" an important factor for you to achieve high Employee Morale? **Yes** or **No** (circle correct answer).

How much would you be willing to sacrifice out of your paycheck per year to observe "better company values within (Company Name)"?

0	1	5	20	50
No	Very little	Moderate amount of	High amount of	A lot of

D.19 Work flexibility

_____37. I am satisfied with the work flexibility provided for my schedule.

_____38. I am able to plan my vacation and take off the days I need.

Is "Work Flexibility" an important factor for you to achieve high Employee Morale? **Yes** or **No** (circle correct answer).

How much would you be willing to sacrifice out of your paycheck per year to have "more work flexibility"?

0	1	5	20	50
No	Very little	Moderate amount of	High amount of	A lot of

Appendix E: Checklist for a great place to work

The purpose of this tool is to assess Employee Morale over your organization. Each set of guidelines will address a particular task, and there are four major parts: (1) Basic Terms of Employment meaning company's compensation policies relating to time and money exchange between the organization and the employees; (2) the Job representing how and when jobs are to be done and who is to do them; (3) Workplace Rules; and (4) stake in Success. Every category should be scored based on the following scale:

0	0.25	0.5	0.75	1
Not at all	Sometimes	Regularly	Frequently	Always

Basic terms of employment

1. Fair pay and benefits:
    a. Compare well with similar employers
    b. Square with company's ability to pay
2. Commitment to job security
3. Commitment to safe and attractive working environment

The job

1. Maximizes individual responsibility for how job is done
2. Flexibility about working hours
3. Opportunities for growth:
    a. Promotes from within
    b. Provides training
    c. Recognizes mistakes as part of learning

Workplace rules

1. Reduces social and economic distinctions between management and other employees
2. Right to due process
3. Right to information
4. Right to free speech
5. Right to confront those in authority
6. Right not to be part of the family/team

Stake in success

1. Shares rewards from productivity improvements
2. Shares profits
3. Shares ownership
4. Shares recognition

NOTE: A great workplace cannot be equated with the presence or absence of a particular set of policies or practices. The quality of the relationship between a company and its employees is instrumental for the success of any organization.

Appendix F: OSHA ergonomic and safety guidelines assessment

The purpose of this tool is to assess OSHA Ergonomic and Safety Guidelines over any organization. Each set of guidelines will address a particular task, and there are three major parts: (1) program management recommendations for management practices addressing ergonomic hazards in the industry or task; (2) worksite analysis recommendations for worksite/workstation analysis techniques geared to the specific operations that are present in the industry or task; and (3) hazard control recommendations that contain descriptions of specific jobs and detail the hazards associated with the operation, possible approaches to controlling the hazard, and the effectiveness of each control approach.

1. To what extent does your ergonomics program address the ergonomic hazards in your industry or task?

0	0.25	0.5	0.75	1
Not at all	Sometimes	Regularly	Frequently	Always

2. Do you have specific hazards as regular working conditions in your industry or task? (0) Y   (1) N (circle correct answer).
3. To what extent does your ergonomics program address the specific control methods that are available for the ergonomic hazards present in your industry?

0	0.25	0.5	0.75	1
Not at all	Sometimes	Regularly	Frequently	Always

4. To what extent does your ergonomics program include a mechanism for reporting injuries, symptoms, and hazards which may be related to ergonomics in the workplace?

0	0.25	0.5	0.75	1
Not at all	Sometimes	Regularly	Frequently	Always

5. Are you responding to these reports? (1) Y   (0) N
6. To what extent does your ergonomics program reflect a process for evaluating the nature and causes of injuries which may be related to ergonomics in the workplace?

0	0.25	0.5	0.75	1
Not at all	Sometimes	Regularly	Frequently	Always

7. Do you have a process for identifying, implementing, and evaluating measures to reduce injuries? (1) Y   (0) N
8. Do you have quantitative data or other information demonstrating the program's provisions effectiveness in reducing the number of ergonomic hazards or the number and severity of workplace injuries related to ergonomics? (1) Y   (0) N
9. Are exits properly identified and lighted, and are exit paths clear?

0	0.25	0.5	0.75	1
Never	Sometimes	Regularly	Frequently	Always

10. Is the emergency lighting operable?

0	0.25	0.5	0.75	1
Never	Sometimes	Regularly	Frequently	Always

11. Has the fire alarm been tested?

0	0.25	0.5	0.75	1
Never	Sometimes	Regularly	Frequently	Always

12. Are portable fire extinguishers available? Are extinguishers serviced/tagged annually?

0	0.25	0.5	0.75	1
Never	Sometimes	Regularly	Frequently	Always

13. Is the sprinkler system operable and tested regularly?

0	0.25	0.5	0.75	1
Never	Sometimes	Regularly	Frequently	Always

14. Are combustibles and trash controlled?

0	0.25	0.5	0.75	1
Not at all	Sometimes	Regularly	Frequently	Always

15. Is lighting protection installed on towers, steeples, or spires?

0	0.25	0.5	0.75	1
Not at all	Sometimes	Regularly	Frequently	Always

16. Has a licensed electrician inspected the electrical wiring?

0	0.25	0.5	0.75	1
Never	Sometimes	Regularly	Frequently	Always

17. Are state inspection certificates on file and current?

0	0.25	0.5	0.75	1
Not at all	Sometimes	Regularly	Frequently	Always

18. Is there a preventive maintenance service contract in effect on heating/air-conditioning equipment?

0	0.25	0.5	0.75	1
Not at all	Sometimes	Regularly	Frequently	Always

19. Is exterior illumination adequate? Are all lights functioning?

0	0.25	0.5	0.75	1
Not at all	Sometimes	Regularly	Frequently	Always

Index